HUGO VON HOFMANNSTHAL
STUDIES IN COMPARISON

HUGO VON HOFMANNSTHAL
STUDIES IN COMPARISON

ALEXANDER STILLMARK

Ariadne Press

Hugo von Hofmannsthal: Studies in Comparison
Alexander Stillmark
© 2024 Alexander Stillmark

Published by Ariadne Press
Riverside, CA

978-1-57241-224-8 hardcover
978-1-57241-225-5 ebook

Publisher's Cataloging-in-Publication data
Names: Stillmark, Alexander, author.
Title: Hugo von Hofmannsthal : studies in comparison /
Alexander Stillmark.
Description: Includes bibliographical references. |
Riverside CA: Ariadne Press, 2024.
Identifiers: LCCN: 2023916200 | ISBN: 978-1-57241-
224-8 (hardcover) | 978-1-57241-225-5 (ebook)
Subjects: LCSH Hofmannsthal, Hugo von,
1874-1929--Criticism and interpretation. | Authors,
Austrian--20th century. | BISAC LITERARY CRITICISM
/ European / General
Classification: LCC PT2617.O47 .S85 2023 | DDC
831/.9/12--dc23

Ariadne Press | Riverside, California

CONTENTS

List of abbreviations to works by and about Yeats
Abbreviations: Editions, Correspondence, Journals
7 – 11

The Significance of Novalis for Hofmannsthal
12 – 49

W. B. Yeats and Hofmannsthal as Exponents of Lyrical Drama
50 – 79

Variants of Social Comedy: Chekhov and *Der Schwierige*
80 – 112

Hofmannsthal and Oscar Wilde
113 – 135

The Poet and His Public. Hofmannsthal's "Ideal Listener"
136 – 162

List of Abbreviations

To works by and about Yeats

Au	*Autobiographies*, London: Macmillan, 1955
E & I	*Essays and Introductions*, London: Macmillan, 1961
Ex	*Explorations: Selected by Mrs. W. B. Yeats*, London: Macmillan, 1962
IR	*W. B. Yeats: Interviews and Recollections*, ed. E H Mikhail 2 vols, London: Macmillan, 1977
IY	Richard Ellman, *The Identity of Yeats*, London: Macmillan, 1954
JBY	*J. B. Yeats: Letters to his Son W. B. Yeats and Others 1868-1922*, ed. with a Memoir by Joseph Hone London: Secker & Warburg, 1983
L	*The Letters of W. B. Yeats*, ed. Allan Wade, London: Hart-Davis, 1954
M	Yeats, *Mythologies*, London: Macmillan, 1959
Me	Yeats, *Memoirs: Autobiography – First Draft Journal*, London: Macmillan, 1972
P	*The Collected Poems of W. B. Yeats*, 2nd ed with later Poems added, London: Macmillan, 1950
Pl	Yeats, *The Collected Plays*, 2nd ed. with additional plays, London: Macmillan, 1952
SR	Yeats, *The Secret Rose and other Stories*, London: Macmillan, 1959
UP	*Uncollected Prose*, collected and edited by John P. Payne and Colton Johnson, 2 vols., London: Macmillan, 1970-1975
VP	*Variorum Edition of the Poems of W. B. Yeats*, edited by Peter Allt and Russell K. Alspach, London: Palgrave Macmillan, 1966
VPl	*Variorum Edition of the Plays of W. B. Yeats*, edited by Russell K. Alspach, London: Macmillan, 1966

Editions

HKA	Hugo von Hofmannsthal, *Sämtliche Werke* ed. Rudolf Hirsch ed l., 37 vols. Frankfurt am Main 1975
GW	Hugo von Hofmannsthal, *Gesammelte Werke in zehn Einzelbänden*, ed. Bernd Schoeller in consultation with Rudolf Hirsch, Frankfurt am Main, 1979-1980
	Gesammelte Werke in Einzelausgaben, ed. Herbert Steiner, 15 vols., Frankfurt am Main, 1945-1959
A	*Aufzeichnungen* 1959
D I	*Dramen* I, 1953
D II	*Dramen* II, 1954
D III	*Dramen* III, 1957
D IV	*Dramen* IV, 1958
E	*Die Erzählungen*, 1968
GLD	*Gedichte und lyrische Dramen* 1946
L I	*Lustspiele* I, 1959
L II	*Lustspiele* II, 1948
L III	*Lustspiele* III, 1956
L IV	*Lustspiele* IV, 1956
P I	*Prosa* I, 1956
P II	*Prosa* II, 1959
P III	*Prosa* III, 1964
P IV	*Prosa* IV, 1966

Correspondence

Br. I   Hugo von Hofmannsthal, *Briefe 1890-1901*, ed. Heinrich Zimmer, Berlin 1935

Br. II   Hugo von Hofmannsthal, *Briefe 1900-1909*, Vienna 1937

H/Almanach 87   ALMANACH, Hugo von Hofmannsthal, *Briefwechsel* mit Max Rychner, Samuel und Hedwig Fischer, Oscar Bie und Moritz Heimann, ed. Claudia Metz-Rychner et al., Frankfurt am Main, 1973

H/Andrian   Hugo von Hofmannsthal – Leopold von Andrian *Briefwechsel* ed. Eugene Weber, Frankfurt am Main, 1972

H/Beer-Hofmann   Hugo von Hofmannsthal – Richard Beer-Hofmann, *Briefwechsel* ed. Eugene Weber, Frankfurt am Main, 1972

H/Bodenhausen   Hugo von Hofmannsthal – Eberhard von Bodenhausen, *Briefe der Freundschaft*, ed. Dora von Bodenhausen, Berlin, 1953

H/Borchardt   Hugo von Hofmannsthal – Rudolf Borchardt, *Briefwechsel*, ed. Marie Luise Borchardt and Herbert Steiner, Frankfurt am Main, 1954

H/Burckhardt   Hugo von Hofmannsthal – Carl J. Burckhardt, *Briefwechsel* ed. Carl J. Burckhardt, Frankfurt am Main, 1956

H/Degeneld   Hugo von Hofmannsthal – Ottnie Grafin Degenfeld, *Briefwechsel*, ed. Marie Therese Miller-Degenfeld und Eugene Weber, zweite verbesserte und vermehrte Auflage, Frankfurt am Main 1974

H/George   *Briefwechsel zwischen George und Hofmannsthal*, ed. Robert Boehringer, zweite ergänzte Auflage Berlin, 1953

H/Haas	Hugo von Hofmannsthal – Willy Haas, *Ein Briefwechsel*, ed. Rolf Italiaander, Berlin 1968
H/Karg	Hugo von Hofmannsthal – Edgar Karg von Bebenburg, *Briefwechsel*, ed. Mary E. Gilbert, Frankfurt am Main, 1966
H/Kessler	Hugo von Hofmannsthal – Harry Graf Kessler, *Briefwechsel 1898-1929*, ed. Hilde Burger, Frankfurt am Main, 1968
H/Mell	Hugo von Hofmannsthal – Max Mell, *Briefwechsel*, ed. Margaret Dietrich und Heinz Kindermann Heidelberg, 1982
H/Nostitz	Hugo von Hofmannsthal – Helene von Nostitz, *Briefwechsel*, ed. Oswald von Nostitz, Frankfurt am Main, 1965
H/Redlich	Hugo von Hofmannsthal – Josef Redlich *Briefwechsel*, ed. Helga Fußgänger, Frankfurt am Main, 1971
H/Rilke	Hugo von Hofmannsthal – Rainer Maria Rilke, *Briefwechsel 1899-1925*, ed. Rudolf Hirsch und Ingeborg Schnack, Frankfurt am Main, 1978
H/Schmujlow	Ria Schmujlow-Claassen un Hugo von Hofmannsthal, *Briefe, Aufsätze, Dokumente*, ed. Claudia Abrecht, Marbach am Neckar, 1982
H/Schnitzler	Hugo von Hofmannsthal – Arthur Schnitzler, *Briefwechsel*, ed. Therese Nickl und Heinrich Schnitzler, Frankfurt am Main, 1983
H/Strauss	Richard Strauss Hugo von Hofmannsthal, *Briefwechsel* ed. Franz und Alice Strauss, revised by Willi Schuh, Zurich, 1955
H/Wildgans	Hugo von Hofmannsthal – Anton Wildgans, *Briefwechsel*, E. Norbert Altenhofer, Heidelberg, 1971
H/Zifferer	Hugo von Hofmannsthal – Paul Zifferer, *Briefwechsel*, ed. Hilde Burger, Vienna, 1983

Journals

CG	*Colloquia Germanica*
CL	*Comparative Literature*
DVLG	*Deutsche Vierteljahrsschrift für Literaturwissenschaft und Geistesgeschichte*
EG	*Etudes germaniques*
Euph	*Euphorion*
GQ	*Germanic Quarterly*
GLL	*German Life and Letters*
GR	*Germanic Review*
HB	*Hofmannsthal-Blätter*
HF	*Hofmannsthal-Forschungen*
JDSG	*Jahrbuch der deutschen Schillergesellschaft*
MAL	*Modern Austrian Literature*
MLR	*Modern Language Review*
Mo	*Monatshefte*
NDR	*Neue deutsche Rundschau*
NR	*Die Neue Rundschau*
OL	*Orbis Literarum*
PEGS	*Publications of the English Goethe Society*
PMLA	*Publications of the Modern Language Association of America*
SD	*Sprache und Dichtung*
WW	*Wirkendes Wort*

THE SIGNIFICANCE OF NOVALIS FOR HOFMANNSTHAL

Wie kann der Mensch Sinn fur etwas haben wenn er nicht den Keim davon in sich hat?

—Novalis

Any broad consideration of the literary relations between Hofmannsthal and Novalis must involve some preliminary comment on the larger question of how Hofmannsthal, that most tradition-conscious of modern writers, viewed German Romanticism.[1] It is well attested that the precocious young Loris was an avid reader, a self-assured "Literat" (man of letters), steeped

---

1   Editions of Novalis referred to: *Schriften: Die Werke Friedrichs von Hardenberg*, herausgegeben von Paul Kluckhohn und Richard Samuel, 4 vols. Stuttgart: Kohlhammer, 1960-1975, abbreviated as SI-IV. Though the names of Novalis and Hofmannsthal have quite frequwntly been brought together and individual points of contact have on occasions received comment, more inclusive and searching critical appraisals are still lacking. Earlier notable contributions to our topic include: Walthr Rehm, *Orpheus: Der Dichter und die Toten*, Dusseldorf: Schwann, 1950, pp. 381-386; L. Pesch, Die Romantische Rebellion in der modernen LIteratur und Kunst, Munich, 1962, pp. 93-101, 104-109; W Vortriede, Novalis und die franzosischen Symbolisten, Stuttgart, 1963, pp. 84-86; W. Paulsen ed., Das Nachleben der Romantik in der modernen deutschen Literatur, Heidelberg 1969, pp. 53-70, 116-129. N. Saul, "Hofmannsthal and Novalis," ed. G. J. Carr et al., Fin-de-Siecle Vienna, Dublin, 1985 attempts to show Hofmannsthal's "lingering yet ambiguous regard for Novalis" and oscillates uneasily between the merely informative and the speculative without entirely satisfying at the critical or evaluative level.

in and critically responsive to the literature of the past. It is clear also from his letters and early prose that he had acquired a facility in forming synthetic judgments on matters of taste and aesthetics. His early essays abound in graceful generalizations and value judgments. Though he, like many more of his generation who were dubbed "Neo-Romantics" at the time, had learned his art of the French Symbolists and had developed techniques which derived from literary Impressionism, it may come as a surprise to find Hofmannsthal quite decisively denouncing Romanticism in a review of Hermann Bahr's *Die Mutter* (1891) when he was just seventeen:

> Denn Romantik ist ja gar nichts Selbständiges, sie ist Krankheit der reinen Kunst, wie der Dilettantismus, das Anempfindungsvermögen, Krankheit des Empfindungsvermögens ist, Und die beiden, Romantik und Dilettantismus, sind immer zusammengegangen. (PI, 17)[2]

> (For Romanticism is not something independent, it is the infirmity of pure art, just as dilettantism, or borrowed sensibility, is infirmity of sensibility. And these two, Romanticism and dilettantism, have always gone together).

It must be noted that Hofmannsthal here understands "Romantik" more broadly as an aesthetic concept, a perennial mode of writing rather than an historical phenomenon with its

---

[2] The connection between dilettantism and the lack of moral seriousness is further illustrated in Hofmannsthal's aphorism: "Im Diletantismus ist der Keim einer sitlichen Verdebnis" (A, 65 In dilettantism there lies the germ of moral decay).

specific theoretical and formal preoccupation. Given the inclusiveness of the idea, he attaches to it a number of qualities such as willful virtuosity, dilettantism and sensationalism, all of which are negative evaluations. The notion that Romanticism exists at one remove from reality, that it represents studied artistry and that it lacks seriousness may all be deduced from this premise.

In his first essay on D'Annunzio (1893) Hofmannsthal associates the notion of "Romantik" with certain intellectual symptoms of the early nineteenth century such as the suspect desire to appear "modern," fervent adulation of religious art which was anyhow understood and a general tendency "sich nach dem 'Naiven' zu sehnen" (PI, 149 to yearn for the "naive"). He also betrays a critical tone in his identification of the twin trends of contemporary Modernism: "die Analyse des Lebens und die Flucht aus dem Leben" (PI, 149 the analysis of life and the scape from life). One can scarcely fail to notice the strong reservations the young writer already harbors about all pretentious individualism, all avant-guardist posturing which seeks to draw attention to itself at all costs:

> Man treibt Anatomie des eigenen Seelenlebens, oder man träumt. Reflexion oder Phantasie, Spiegelbild oder Traumbild. Modern sind alte Möbel und junge Nervositäten. Modern ist das psychologische Graswachsenhören und das Plätschern in der reinphantastischen Wunderwelt.

> (One pursues the anatomy of one's inner life or else one dreams. Cogitation or fantasy, mirror-image or dream-image, The Modern consists in antique furniture

and youthful neuroses. The Modern consists in psychological hearing-the-grass-grow and plashing sound of the purely fantastic world of marvels).

This setting of the contemporary manner of perception against an outmoded and suspect world of experience marks Hofmannsthal out as a modern whose critical consciousness unavoidably opens up a gulf between him and historical Romanticism. A letter to his friend Richard Beer-Hoffmann (May 14, 1895) makes this position clear:

> Wir sind zu kritisch um in einer Traumwelt zu leben, wie die Romantiker; mit unseren schweren Köpfen brechen wir immer durch das dünne Medium, wie schwere Reiter auf Moorboden. Es handelt sich freilich immer nur darum ringsum an den Grenzen des Gesichtskreises Potemkin'sche Dörfer aufzustellen, aber solche an die man selber glaubt.[3]

(We are too critical to live in a dream world as the Romantics did; with our heavy heads we keep breaking through the thin medium like heavy riders on marshy land. It is, of course, always a question od setting up Potemkin villages round about the borders of our vision, but only such as one believes in oneself.)

And he continues later in the same letter; "Wie kann es recht sein, sich um viele Dinge nicht zu kümmern, da doch alle Dinge gleich richtig und groß sind (was die Romantiker so widerlich ignoriert haben?)" (How can it be right to be unconcerned about many things, when all things are equally right and

---

[3] Hugo von Hofmannsthal to Beer-Hofmann, H/Beer-Hofmann 1, Br. 1, p. 130.

great [which the Romantics so nauseatingly ignored]). What the young Hofmannsthal is so strongly objecting to is the Romantics' obdurate eclecticism, a disposition to dismiss from mind so much in reality that has proper claim on our intelligence and sympathies, a readiness to pass autonomous judgment on the relative importance of things. It is the artificial selectivity of the aesthetic existence which Hofmannsthal condemns, (though, as is known, he was himself all too readily identified with such a position). His metaphor of "Potemkin'sche Dörfer" in fact stands for deliberate self-delusion; the kind of counterfeit existence of self-isolation which one finds in the figures of Claudio and the "Kaufmannssohn" (merchant's son); both depictions of that disregard for wholeness of experience which attracts their author's moral censure.

The undeniable reservations Hofmannsthal felt towards Romanticism as an intellectual movement persisted throughout his life as two further instances from his writing in mid-life and his last years will serve to show. The first, a diary entry for November 23, 1906, records his wish to write an essay which would dispense with the concept of Romanticism as being too inclusive and undifferentiated to be meaningful:

> Mit dem Worte Romantik haben die Dichter jener Epoche sich selbst eine Atmosphäre suggeriert, worin aber das worauf es einzig ankommt, das Einzelne, Nie-Wiederkehrende, das Besonderste verschleiert wird. Das Vage, Unzulängliche, in allem Gleiche, das Unbestimmte, das worüber sich viele verständigen konnten, drängt sich vor und verschleiert die Idee jedes Einzelnen. (A, 156)

(With the term Romanticism, the poets of that age managed to suggest to themselves an atmosphere wherein the sole significant factor, the singular, the never-to-be-repeated, the most particular thing, is blurred. That which is vague, insufficient, ever the same, the uncertain, the thing on which many could agree, asserts itself and blurs the idea of each individual).

Hofmannsthal's fine estimation of personal achievement in literature, his interest in individual intellect and style prompted him to turn away from the generalized view and blanket judgment when it came to treating so complex a phenomenon as Romanticism. He was not so much absorbed by Romantic philosophy or theorizing as drawn by individual works of genius from the period.[4] In assessing creative talent, the particular instance of excellence was ultimately more significant to him than the general intellectual climate in which it arose. The second example is to be found among his notes for an essay "Über Walther Brecht" (1926) where he identifies a particular intellectual weakness attributable to the Romantics: "Gefahren des Geistigen, das bloße Velleität bleibt, wie vieles von den Romatikern" (PIV, 320 Perils of the intellect which remains mere velleity, as so much by the Romantics). The key term is "Velleität": the act of merely willing or desiring, that characteristic Romantic yearning for an infinite goal implying a state of mind which finds pleasure in the very act of yearning, not of attainment. The dangers of falling victim to

---

4 It is noteworthy that Hofmannsthal included in his anthology *Deutsche Erzähler* (1912) twenty works of narrative fiction, about half of which belonged to Romanticism. Though he had considered including *Die Lehrlinge zu Sais*, Novalis was not, in the end, part of this selection.

Romantic velleity, that "namenloses Sehnen" (unknown yearning) one encounter is parts of the early lyrical period, are recorded form the vantage point of maturity of course. The poet Loris had not been free of such indefinite longing.[5] The subsequent insight and apprehension may in part have been prompted by recollections of a former self that had known the lure of "die blaue Blume" (the blue flower).

If specific aspects of German Romanticism troubled and alienated Hofmannsthal, the figure of Novalis occupied a special place for him among the generation of writers born in the 1770's. Only Hölderlin and Kleist were held in comparable esteem by him. It is interesting to note that Hofmannsthal does not view Novalis in solely representative terms as the Romantic *par excellence*, which is a conventional view, but reverses the terms: "In Novalis ist Romantik, also beginnendes 19. Jahrhundert. Es ist darin aber auch der zarteste Blütenstaub des 18., im Moment des Verwehens" (A, 192 In Novalis there is Romanticism, namely, the incipient 19th century. In it, however, is also the most delicate pollen of the 18th century at the moment of its dispersal). The idea that Romanticism constitutes only a part of Novalis the writer and thinker, and that he has a significance which transcends its horizons, is crucial. He is seen as a transitional figure representing the last vestiges of eighteenth-century thought and sensibility as well as the nucleus of future developments. Hofmannsthal's metaphor

---

5 See for example "Erlebnis" (GLD, 11, "Dein Antlitz…" (GLD, 15), "Was die Braut geträumt hat" (GLD, 116), *Der Tor und der Tod* (GLD, 271, or the reminiscence *Raoul Richter* (PIII, 170).

of pollination which derives from Novalis, where it abounds, is used to suggest the rich fruitfulness of his subsequent influence.

Hofmannsthal was wont to single out and evaluate individual writers of genius for the uniqueness of their contribution to the German language. As he wrote in 1927: "Unsere höchsten Dichter allein, möchte man sagen, gebrauchen unsere Sprache sprachgemäß – ob auch die Schriftsteller, bleibt schon fraglich": (P IV, 437 Our greatest poets alone, one is tempted to say, employ our language according to its genius – whether our writers do so too, remains dubious). He believed that German lacked a continuous, coherent literary tradition and could boast only a number of supreme isolated literary achievements: "Wir haben seit hundertfünfzig Jahren eine neue dichterische Sprache, viele große Dichter und einzelne große Schriftsteller, aber wir haben streng genommen nicht, was man eine Literatur nennen kann" (P III, 429 For the past 150 years we have had a new literary language, many great poets and great individual writers, but we do not have, strictly speaking, what may be termed a literature).[6] Novalis was for him decidedly among those German writers who possessed original genius and had made a major contribution to the literary language. The association in his mind between this idea of the solitary literary talent in contention with the German language and the unique value of Novalis's achievement is made explicit in the diary entry for January 27, 1928:

---

6 Hofmannsthal saw himself as the torch-bearer of tradition and repeated used this metaphor (A, 201, 205, 296).

Ja, die Franzosen, die Spanier, Die Engländer, alle Andern haben was wir nicht haben: eine literarische Tradition, eine Entwicklung des Urteils von einer Generation zur anderen, kurz eine wirkliche Literatur. Wir haben nur Ansätze und immer wieder Ansätze, freilich sind sie oft genialer als die Werke der Andern, aber zum Werk oder gar zur Kette von Werken kommt es bei uns höchst selten. Eine literarische Erscheinung wie Novalis und ihr Wert, der in einem gewissen Betracht unschätzbar ist, ist einem Nicht-Deutschen gar nicht klarzumachen. Er ist mehr das Ingrediens einer potentiellen etwa zu realisierenden Literatur als das Bestandstück einer wirklichen. (A, 193)

(Indeed, the French, the Spanish, the English, all the others have what we do not have: a literary tradition, a growth in judgment from one generation to the next, in short, a proper literature. We have beginnings and ever new beginnings; true, they often show more genius than the works of others, but we very rarely achieve a work, much less a whole series of works. A literary phenomenon such as Novalis and its value, which is in a certain sense incalculable, simply cannot be made clear to a non-German. He is more the ingredient of a potential literature which has still to be realized, than the composite part of an actual literature).

Novalis is seen as one of those significant beginnings ("Ansätze") in the course of German literature which know no succession. To Hofmannsthal he appears more in the nature of a catalyst to later developments, an incitement to intellect and imagination, rather than a creator of form and paradigm in literature. That is doubtless why he finds the metaphor of seed and pollination particularly apposite: the collection *Blütenstaub*

(*Pollen*) especially was to prove a fruitful source of intellectual stimulus to Hofmannsthal in maturer years. The fact too that Novalis left the greater part of his oeuvre uncompleted and as paralipomena or "Fragments" also shows something of a parallel with Hofmannsthal, who likewise left a vast store of unfinished work to posterity. This includes numerous plans, sketches, notes and ideas stemming from a comparatively fertile mind and one that could not always find the form that was adequate to a conception. This phenomenon of a mind teeming with more ideas than it can formally master and execute is perhaps one of the more basic links between the two writers. The full extent of Hofmannsthal's unfinished oeuvre is still to be evaluated when the historical-critical edition is finished, and the unexpected discovery in Cracow of hundreds of unpublished manuscripts by Novalis indicates how incomplete a picture we have of his writings even today.

In surveying all the points of reference to Novalis in Hofmannsthal's published work and his letters, one can identify a pattern which suggest a distinct development from spontaneous and unconscious assimilation in the early years roughly up to "Ein Brief" ("A Letter") (1902) to an ever deepening intellectual appreciation and conscious appraisal of his significance, more especially as an aphorist. The inclusion of a selection of Novalis's fragments in the first edition of *Deutsches Lesebuch* (*German Reader*) and in his first number of *Neue Deutsche Beiträge* (*New German Contributions*), both published by the Bremer Presse in 1923, the further inclusion of a number of aphorisms in *Buch der Freude* (1926) (*Book of Friends*) and frequent references to Novalis the thinker in the later prose, are clear acknowledgements of an absorbing interest which is to receive comment. Apart from a few intervening years up until 1907, the year of the important public address "Der Dichter und die Zeit" ("The Poet and Time"), the early lyrical works often suggest certain thematic and stylistic affinities with Novalis's writing, but they do so only at the level of implicit reference, literary echo and reminiscence. Hofmannsthal retrospectively acknowledged the early influence on him of Novalis (i.e. approximately from 1892 onward) in a diary entry of the year 1926. But then Novalis is only one of a number of other names from among English and French poets, and he is not given pride of place but mentioned as an afterthought: "ferner: Novalis – die englischen Dichter, besonders Keats" (A, 237 in addition: Novalis – the English poets, especially Keats). In any appraisal of literary influence across the historical divide of the nineteenth century, one cannot ignore the far-reaching differences both social and political, both cultural, philosophical and scientific. The common ground may indeed be literature, yet how far-removed is the confident idealism and strong faith of Novalis from the febrile sensibilities and pervasive skepticism of Hofmannsthal. What Hofmannsthal could most readily relate to in Novalis belonged to the sphere of intellect, to those forms of creative thinking which, since they were intimately bound up with the faculties of intuition and imagination, were congenial to his own.

    Given the complex and hazardous undertaking of tracing those elusive ghosts called "literary influence" in any writer, and particularly in Hofmannsthal who opened up his mind to all

European literature, I propose to evaluate mainly some formal attestations of inner indebtedness for which secure evidence exists. We shall therefore be looking at three principal areas of Hofmannsthal's reception of Novalis: the poet's consciousness of the self and how it is reflected, the role of figurative and symbolic language and the importance of the Fragment; a favorite form of both writers and one which can help us to explore certain characteristic modes of thought in both.

The writings of the younger Hofmannsthal show an insistent preoccupation with the creative self, an ever-changing series of portraits and images representing projections of the artistic consciousness. This self-absorption and self-reflection has most often been seen as a narcissism born of the period, a typical feature of *fin-de-siècle* aestheticism. Yet it can equally be related to Hofmannsthal's early fascination with a central aspect of the writings of Novalis. The figure of the poet as philosopher, priest, lover, magician, prophet and Orphic voice, is given commanding status in Novalis's writings. He is placed at the center of the universe, endowed with godlike powers of omniscience and divination: "Der echte Dichter ist allwissend – er ist eine wirkliche Welt im kleinen" (S II, 592) "Der Dichter bleibt wahr" (S III, 693) "Nur der Künstler kann den Sinn des Lebens errathen" (S III, 562), "Der Poet versteht die Natur besser wie der wissenschaftliche Kopf" (S III, 468).[7] (The true poet is omniscient – he is a

---

7 Walter Naumann has pointed out the crucial significance of Hofmannsthal's self-awareness as a poet: "Dichter zu sein, war ein Kernerlebnis für ihn" (to be a poet was for him a primal experience),

real world in miniature. The poet remains eternally true. Only the artist can divine the meaning of life. The poet understands nature better than the scientific mind). The numerous depictions of and the discourses on the powers of the poet and of poetry in *Heinrich von Ofterdingen*, the ideas proffered in the Fragments, especially the "Poetizismen" (Fragments of Poetics), all convey a potent sense of sovereignty. The sense of being favored, vouchsafed the special gift of poetry, is an essential trait, Klingsohr tells Heinrich: "In der Nähe des Dichters bricht die Poesie überall aus" (SI, 283 poetry breaks out everywhere when the poet is near). Though in essence poetry is a universal gift, as Heinrich is told, – "es ist gar nichts Besonders. Es ist die eigentümliche Handlungsweise des menschlichen Geistes: (SI, 287 It is nothing at all unusual. It is the mode of behavior peculiar to the human mind) – it is raised in fact to the high principle of truth and confers upon the poet the privileges of illumination and insight. Novalis presents the poet as a microcosm of the universe; and it is the special efficacy of poetry that it offers not only knowledge of the world but self-knowledge. In *Blütenstaub* we find the words: "Nach innen geht der geheimnisvolle Weg. In uns oder nirgends ist die Ewigkeit mit ihren Welten, die Vergangenheit und die Zukunft" (S II, 419 The mysterious path leads inwards, Nowhere but in ourselves is eternity with all its worlds, the past and the future). This is paralleled by Hofmannsthal's self-analytical note: "Die Introversion als Weg in die Existenz. (Der mystische Weg)"

"Hofmannsthals Auffassung von seiner Sendung als Dichter" Mo vol. 39, no. 3, 1947, pp. 184-187.

(A, 215 Introversion is the path into existence [the mystical path]). Though ostensibly complementary as statements about the poet's self-determined path, there are significant distinctions to be made. For Hofmannsthal, the product of the scientific age, "Introversion" assumes a meaning that involves psychological complexities and uncertainties not to be found in Novalis. The strong personal conviction that expresses itself in Novalis's assertive statement above all distinguishes it from Hofmannsthal who is, by contrast, most tentative in sketching his own development in retrospect, The phrase "der mystische Weg" strikes one as a figurative approximation and hardly carries the transcendental meaning of Novalis's "Die künftige Welt" (the future world) within the same Fragment. One is reminded of Max Kommerell's perceptive identification: "übrigens liebt es der Dichter Mysterien zu verweltlichen" (incidentally, this poet is fond of secularizing mysteries).[8] Novalis, here as elsewhere, is self-assured and persuasive in tone; Hofmannsthal is merely suggestive.

For Hofmannsthal, introversion connotes a condition of heightened self-awareness and the early work everywhere shows an uncommon degree of introspective interest and emphasis. He himself speaks of "das Motif des Zu-sich-selber-kommens in den Jugendwerken" (A, 219 the motif of finding oneself in the youthful works). His writing evolves through a protean array of poetic personae who represent variations of an experience for which Hofmannsthal tentatively used the term "Praeexistenz" (preexistence) which he qualified in *Ad me ipsum* as "glorreicher, aber

---

8 Max Kommerell, "Nachlese der Gedichte 1934" NR 3-4, 1954, p. 570.

gefährlicher Zustand" (A, 213 glorious yet perilous condition). The notion of anamnesis is perhaps not so much believed in as adduced as an expedient to communicate the mysterious quality of personal illumination and sense of timelessness involved in the experience.[9] Hofmannsthal also resorts to Novalis's favorite term "Magie: in expressing that ecstasy of the mind in which all things appear harmoniously united. "Der Anfang ist pure Magie: Praeexistenz" (A, 238 The beginning is pure magic: preexistence). He pointedly refers to "Novalis der Magier" (Novalis the Magician) in an essay of 1908 (P II, 343). The poem "Ein Traum von großer Magie" ("A dream of mighty magic") offers a vision of the "Magier" whose powers defy all material limitations of space and time, who can feel one with the elements and the human life:

> Er fühlte traumhaft aller Menschen Los.
> So wie er seine eignen Glieder fühlte.
> Ihm war nichts nah und fern, nichts klein und groß.
> (GLD, 22)[10]
> (Dreamlike he felt the lot of all mankind,
> As he could feel the limbs he owned.
> Nothing to him seems hear or far, nor small nor great.)

The conclusion to the poem suggests identification of the spiritual part of man – "unser Geist" (our mind) – and the

---

9 David H. Miles in his excellent study Hofmannsthal's Novel Andreas: Memory and Self, Princeton: Princeton University Press, 1972, p. 18 makes the point that Hofmannsthal's Neoplatonic view of memory "is essentially anti-Platonic" for unlike traditional Platonism, Hofmannsthal "continually stresses the concrete immanence of recollection."
10 Hofmannsthal also refers to the mysterious powers of poetic language as "diese stumme Magie" (this speechless magic) in "Der Dichter und diese Zeit" (PII, 240, 241).

sovereign powers of the "Magier." Poet and magician are one, or in Novalis's words, "der Zauberer ist poet" (S II, 591 the magician is poet). For Novalis "der magische Idealist" (magic idealist) is the firm believer in a supernatural order to which access may be gained by schooling the will to make the spiritual part dictate to the material, the mind to govern matter, in order to bring about the realization of the idea ("Realisation der Idee"). "Magie ist gleich Kunst, die Sinnenwelt willkührlich zu gebrauchen" (S II, 546; "Alle Erfahrung ist Magie – nur magisch erklärbar: (S, III, 401 Magic resembles the art of using the realm of the senses at will; all experience is magic – only explicable by magic).[11] This crucial element of Novalis; thought, it seems to me, partakes of both the irrational and the psychological spheres, and its appeal for the young Hofmannsthal is understandable, as he writes approvingly of intuitive knowledge and illumination (e. g. in "Erlebnis": Obgleich ichs nicht begreife, doch ich wußt es" (GLD, 10 "Experience": although I do not grasp it, yet I knew it). Yet what engaged Hofmannsthal was not so much the schooling of the will to transcend and command the material world but the exercise of his power over words: "Die magische Herrschaft über das Wort und das Bild als Zeichen" (A, 215 the magical command of word, image, sign). The dangerous ambivalence of "Praeexistenz," this condition of spiritual elation which gives rise to "Wortmagie"

---

11 For B. Haywood magic idealism means "essentially nothing more than metaphorical representation" which might indeed be seen as a salutary simplification if it did not cut away essential element of Romantic idealism and perceptionism from Novalis's though, *Novalis: The Veil of Imagery*, 's-Gravenhage: Mouton, 1959, p. 10.

(word-magic), is repeatedly acknowledged and formulated. The point is that it represents a temporary condition: it is a privileged moment. For all its preciousness, it is transient and that makes it appear precarious or illusory.

Novalis represents the gift of poetry in his symbolic novel *Heinrich von Ofterdingen* as a constant and secure possession which unfolds effortlessly with every new experience: "Alles was er sah und hörte, schien nur neue Riegel in ihm wegzuschieben und neue Fenster ihm zu öffnen" (SI, 268 Everything he saw and heard seemed to draw aside new bolts and to open new windows within him). A law of spontaneity is alive in the poet; just as his understanding is unlocked by each new encounter so the meaning of nature is opened up for him. In him the Romantic ideal of "Universalpoesie" (universal poetry) is realized. Hofmannsthal's poetry of "erhöhte Augenbicke" (heightened moments), on the other hand, represents a dangerous lure which offers semblances rather than essences and is beset with doubt and disappointments. So much of this poetry and the lyrical dramas display the problematical self of the poet; poems like "Psyche," "Brief," "Sünde des Lebens," "Der Schatten eines Toten" ("Psyche, " "Letter," "Sin of Life," "The Shadow of a Dead Man") all delve into the questionableness of the poet's craft. The dangers of solipsism are made present in most of the principle figures of the lyrical dramas, especially Andrea, Claudio and Elis. The threat of isolation and severance from the real world of experience is a constant theme. It is often the loss of unity, indeed the loss of faith in creativity which intrudes. The dramatic monologue "Der Jüngling und die

Spinne" ("The Youth and the Spider") might be taken as paradigmatic within this context, as it explores the abrupt conversion of the mind from the state of euphoric oneness with world – "Wie ich nun de Welt besitze/Ist über alle Worte, alle Träume" (How I now posses the world/is far beyond all words, all dreams) – to cold realization of life's remorseless indifference and cruelty:

> Die Welt besitzt sich selber, O ich lerne!
> Nicht hemme ich die widrige Gestalt
> So wenig als den Lauf der schönen Sterne. (GLD, 36 f)
>
> ("The world possesses its own self, O I begin to learn!
> No more can I prevent this hideous shape
> Than halt the lovely stars upon their course).

The knowledge gained by this recoiling from ugliness and death is just one instance of that pattern of insight into the blight of aesthetic self-indulgence we repeatedly encounter, most notably in *Der Tor und der Tod*. Excessive preoccupation with aesthetic pleasure and the refinement of the sensibilities entails the loss of "Bindung" and "Beziehung", key concepts in Hofmannsthal and ones which show affinity with Novalis's quest for the restoration of unity between all things. The words that Death speaks to Claudio are at the same time a reiteration of Novalis's philosophy of universal unification:

> Im Innern quilt euch allen treu ein Geist,
> Der diesem Chaos toter Sachen
> Beziehung einzuhauchen heißt. (GLD, 281)
>
> (Within you all a faithful spirit stirs
> Which bids you to inspire with meaning
> This chaos of dead things).

The importance of Novalis as a mind strenuously pursuing the quest for "Beziehung" through his thinking and in his imaginative writing (and here the *Märchen* offered the most fertile medium) is again a crucial link. The very idea of the poet as one who connects, one who can discern "Bezüge" (relations) in the disjunctions of the phenomenal universe is fundamental to Novalis as it is to Hofmannsthal. "Auf Vergleichen, Gleichen läßt sich wohl alles Erkennen, Wissen etc zurückführen" wrote Novalis (S II, 546 all cognition, knowledge etc. may act most likely be traced back to the act of comparing, equating). And in a letter to Friedrich Schlegel, June 8, 1796, he remarked: "Ich fühle in allem immer mehr die erhabenen Glieder eines wunderbaren Ganzen" (I increasingly feel in everything the sublime members of one marvelous whole).

Both writers are remarkable for their use of metaphoric and symbolic language as the principal means of articulating meaning and conveying a wholeness of vision. Novalis remains a symbolist even when he philosophizes. It is to Novalis above all that Hofmannsthal from his beginnings owes his highly developed sense of figurative language and his natural recourse to symbolic statement. The words he wrote of himself in 1894 may stand as a definition of his creative personality: "Ich bin ein Dichter weil ich bildlich erlebe" (A, 107 I am a poet because I experience figuratively). To borrow Middleton Murry's terms in relation to Hofmannsthal, "metaphor becomes almost a mode of apprehension."[12] He once eloquently summarized the illuminating power

---

12 J. Middleton Murry, *The Problem of Style*, London: Oxford University Press, 1967, p. 11.

of the metaphoric in a review of 1894:

> Dieser plötzlich blitzartigen Erleuchtung, in der wir einen Augenblick lang den großen Weltzusammenhang ahnen, schauernd die Gegenwart der Ideen spüren, dieses ganzen mystischen Vorganges, der uns die Metapher leuchtend und real hinterläßt. (PI, 191)

> (this sudden lightning like illumination in which we sense bit for a moment the great unity of the universe, feel with a thrill the presence of the idea, of this entire mystical process which metaphor leaves behind for us, glowing and real).

Metaphor is understood essentially as an instrument of perceptive unification since it fuses the idea with wider intuitive apprehension. The facility for thinking in metaphor distinguishes not just the young Hofmannsthal but is an indissoluble part of his creative use of language throughout. The reflections published in *Blätter für die Kunst* (1897 Journals for Art) under the heading "bildlicher Ausdruck" (Metaphoric Expression) contain some of Hofmannsthal's fundamental convictions about the symbolic nature of literature and are close to Novalis both in spirit and form. Figurative expression is said to be "Kern und Wesen aller Poesie: jede Dichtung ist durch und durch ein Gebilde aus uneigentlichen Ausdrücken" (PI, 286 Core and essence of all poetry: every literary work is through and through a composite of non-literal expression). From youth to maturity the conviction remains that the province of poetry is symbolism and that the poet's natural mode of expression is in "unaufhörlichen Gleichnissen" (A, 286 unending allegories). Ruminations on the nature and function of simile stemming from Hofmannsthal's later years continue to revolve about the sense of wholeness which it bestows: "Der magische Grundsatz *pars pro toto* in den Gleichnissen wirksam" (A, 199 the magic principal *pars pro toto* effective in the allegories).

The numerous fragments in which Novalis speculated on figurative language, cipher and symbol, and which Bruce Heywood has so lucidly commentated, are not merely investigation into the expressiveness of language but also a reflection of "his belief in the metaphorical character of the world and of life itself."[13] It is a belief that might be summarized in Goethe's words "alles Vergängliche ist nur ein Gleichnis" (all that is transcient is but a parable). Hofmannsthal's indebtedness to Novalis does not embrace the latter's Neoplatonic world-view but is limited to the province of language in its symbolic potential. The opening passage of *Die Lehrlinge zu Sais* (*The Apprentices at Sais*), in which Novalis refers to "Jene große Chriffrenschrift" (that great script in ciphers) permeating all natural phenomena, conjures up the visible universe as the mysterious hieroglyph signifying a higher reality. The metaphor of the key, "den Schlüssel dieser Wunderschrift" (the key to this miraculous script), is of crucial significance within Novalis's writings and is perhaps most memorably formulated in the twelve prophetic lines from the second, incomplete part of *Heinrich von Ofterdingen* which begin: "Wenn nicht mehr Zahlen und Figuren/Sind Schlüssel aller Kreaturen" (SI, 344 When numbers and figures no longer feature/As key to

---

13 B. Haywood, op cit., p. 14. See especially the first chapter on "The Nature and Function of Novalis's Imagery."

every living creature). Hofmannsthal borrows the key-metaphor from Novalis in *Ein Brief* but employs it without mystic's belief in a transcendent world:

> Oder es ahnte mir, alles wäre Gleichnis und jede Kreatur ein Schlüssel der andern, und ich fühlte mich wohl den, der imstande wäre, eine nach der andern bei der Krone zu packen und mit ihr so viele der andern aufzusperren, als sie aufsperren könnte." PII, 10 f)[14]

> (Or again I dimly sensed that all things ere a parable and every creature a key to another, and I felt rather as one who was capable of grasping one after the other by the antlers and thereby of unlocking as many of the others as they could).

What Hofmannsthal is presenting through the person of Chandos is one of those incommunicable "Momente der Erhöhung" (A, 216 heightening powers!) as he called them, momentary illuminations whose religious significance he proceeds to doubt in the very next paragraph. That is why he calls Chandos's predicament "die Situation des Mystikers ohne Mystik" (A, 215 the situation of the mystic without mysticism). Chandos may display an avid "Weltfrömmigkeit" (worldly piety)

---

14 The implicit acknowledgement of Novalis in this crucial essay is clear, as has been recognized by Steven C. Schaber, "Novalis's *Monolog* and Hofmannsthal's *Ein Brief*: Two Poets in Search of a Language," GQ, 47, 1974, Cf. also Hans-Joachim Mähl, "Die Mystik der Worte – Zum Sprachproblem in der modernen deutschen Dichtung," WW 13, 1963, pp. 294, 302, who sees Hofmannsthal's use of the language of mystification as "entromsntisierte Romantik" (deromanticized Romanticism) and as "Säkularisiertes Erbe der Romantik" (secularized legacy of Romanticism).

in Hofmannsthal's words (A, 216) but he has not the religious conviction of a Novalis to sustain a unified vision of life. He points to a diversity of mundane objects and writes. "alles dies kann das Gefäß meiner Offenbarung werden" (PII, 14 everything can become the vessel of my revelation). Using the language of mystical belief he displays his spiritual bereavement. He has lost the ability to assent to that universal symbolism which underlies and unites all things; he merely retains a vague presentiment of it. "Es ist mir dann, als bestünde mein Körper aus lauter Chiffren, die mir alles aufschließen." (PII, 17 it then seems to be as if my body consisted of numerous ciphers which unlock all things for me) he adds in terms which echo Novalis and are an attempt to recapture in language something of that "große Einheit" (great oneness) between the spiritual and the material world which eludes him.[15]

To desire for the restitution of unity is again present in the phrase "mit dem Herzen zu denken" (PI, 17 thinking with the heart) which Chandos proposes as a means of entering into fuller

---

15 According to Rudolf Kassner, Hofmannsthal once used a concept which he termed "Welt hinter der Welt" (a world behind the world) a a means of indicating this unifying principle: "Welt hinter der Welt sei das, was man gelegentlich auch Mythos nenne, wohl auch Konvention, als in welcher sich allemal ein Mythische sich verhärtet hatte, auch so: platt geworden ware" (world behind the world is that which one also on occasion terms myth, perhaps also convention, bing something in which a mythical quality has hardened, or possibly has become matter-of-fact). "Erinnerung an Hugo von Hofmsnnstal," in Helmut A. Fiechtner ed., *Der Dichter im Spiegel der Freunde*, 2nd ed., Berne Munich 1962, p. 250.

communion with all being. This too is derivative of Novalis, who wrote: "Das Herz ist der Schlüssel der Welt und des Lebens: (SII, 606 the heart is the key to the world and to life). A further occurrence of this idea is to be found in *Das Buch der Freunde* where Hofmannsthal notes "Letztes Gewahrwerden der Natur mit dem Herzen: Novalis: (A, 68 last apperception of nature with the heart: Novalis). The interfusion of emotion, intuition and intellect is of course central to Novalis, as it is characteristic of Romantic thought as a whole.[16] Through Chandos, Hofmannsthal offers a very personal exploration of that innermost experience of the poet's mind where symbolism takes form. So much of the perceptual intelligence and linguistic finesse of this famous letter owes a debt to the precedent of Novalis.

A further instance, within the context of symbolism, of Hofmannsthal's evident indebtedness to Novalis occurs in the fictive dialogue "Das Gespräch über Gedichte" ("The Conversation about Poems") written in the following year.[17] It is the point where

---

16 In "Der Dichter im Spiegel der Zeit," Hofmsnnsthsl has expressed this need in a chiastic figure as "fühlendem Denken, denkndem Fühlen" (PII, 242 feeling thought, thinking feeling).
17 It is often overlooked that the Chandos letter, far from being an isolated private confession, forms only part of a series of imagined letters and dialogues written about this time in which Hofmannsthal employs historical or invented characters in order to explore a literary or philosophical yopic. ("Über Charaktere im Roman und im Drama" 1902, "Das Gespräch über Gedichte" 1903, "Dialog über den Tasso von Goethe" 1906, "Unterhaltungen über die Schriften von Keller" 1906, "Unterhaltungen über ein neues Buch" 1906, "Die Briefe des Zurückgekehrten" 1907.) A letter to Leopold von Andrian of January 16, 1902, Br. II, p. 100, speaks of a whole volume to be entitled "Erfundene

Gabriel is discussing the nature of poetic symbols. He proposes that the swans they are watching will, if seen with the eyes of the poet, take on a pristine fullness of meaning:

> Gesehen mit diesen Augen sind die Tiere die eigentlichen Hieroglyphen, sind sie lebendige geheimnisvolle Chiffern, mit denen Gott unsuasprechliche Dinge in die Welt geschrieben hat. Glücklich der Dichter, daß auch er diese göttlichen Chiffern in seine Schrift verweben darf – (PII, 87)

> (Seen with these eyes, the animals are the actual hieroglyphs, they are living, mysterious ciphers, with which God has written ineffable things into this world. How happy is the poet, that he too can weave these divine ciphers into his writing).

The vocabulary of the hieroglyph, cipher and symbol is recognizably derivative of Novalis's thought which identifies true artistic creativity with symbolic statement. "Die erste Kunst ist Hierogyphistik: (SIII, 571 the first of the arts is hieroglyphistics). For Hofmannsthal too the poet is more than a maker of craftsman, as the notable address "Der Dichter und die Zeit" makes plain, but retains some vestige of the visionary that we find in Novalis.[18] Gabriel, speaking largely for Hofmannsthal, says: "Dem Kind ist alles ein Symbol, dem Frommen ist Symbol das einzig Wirkliche, und der Dichter vermag nichts anderes zu erblicken" (PII, 87 to the child everything is a symbol, to the pious person

---

Gespräche und Briefe" (Invented conversations and letters) which Hofmannsthal had planned at the time.
18 For further discussion of this topic see chater 5 above.

the symbol is the sole reality and the poet can see nothing else). The very link itself between the child, the pious mind and the poet, as those who have the most immediate access to symbolism, is a feature of Romantic thought which Hofmannsthal utilizes in order to illustrate the pristine nature and accessibility of the symbol, "das Element der Poesie" (PII, 89 the element of poetry).

Of all the literary forms it is the *Märchen* which offers fullest scope for symbolism. For Novalis it represented "Der Kanon der Poesie" (SIII, 449 the canon of poetry) and most completely embodied his poetics. As a synthesis of Romantic aesthetic theory and praxis, it combined dream with allegory, fantasy with nature philosophy, the marvelous with the symbolic. The prototypes which Novalis left to posterity "Hyazinth und Rosenblüte" and "Klingsohrs Märchen," like Goethe's example, clearly left their imprint on Hofmannsthal's own excursions into the genre. *Das Märchen von der verschleierten Frau* (1900 *The Tale of the Veiled Woman*) and the later *Die Frau ohne Schatten* (1919 *The Woman without a Shadow*) have both motivic and stylistic traits. In the first, Hofmannsthal even pointedly calls his principal figure the "Bergmann" (miner) Hyazinth. The role of memory, the relativization of time, the loss and recovery of self are all shared motifs. Hyazinth's journey to "die verschleierte Jungfrau" (The veiled virgin) Isis are akin to Elis Fröböm's search for "die Bergkönigin" (the mountain queen) or the Kaiserin's search for her shadow, as variants of that "Grundthema: sich selbst finden" (A, 222 Basic theme: to find one's self); all are metaphors for that circuitous and arduous route to vital knowledge of self and world.

Hofmannsthal's language in his unfinished *Märchen* is quite strikingly modeled on Novalis's style, especially in the use of the epithet, its translucent imagery and controlled rhythmic flux.[19] Novalis's sentence "Beiwörter sind dichterische Hauptwörter: (adjectives are the primary words of poetry) obviously went deep with Hofmannsthal.[20] What again distinguishes Hofmannsthal from his model is the increase of complexity and sophistication, the deepening of psychological interest; in general a tendency to suggest meaning darkly as opposed to Novalis's inclination to fabulate and allegorize. The "Märchen" form serves Hofmannsthal as a vehicle for his most intimate concerns as a poet and the

---

19 Merely a sentence such as the following is sufficient to indicate the stylistic indebtedness to *Heinrich von Ofterdingen* and *Die Lehrlinge zu Sais*: "Und aus dem Innersten her durchsetzte ihn ein unnennbares völlig neues und doch überaus bestimmtes Gefühl seiner selbst, in dem alle die früheren ahnungsweise Glücksgefühle enthalten waren, aber nur wie kleine Bläschen, die sich augenblicklich in der kristallenen flutenden leuchtenden Klarheit des Ganzen auflösten" (E, 81 And from his innermost being an inexpressible, wholly new, yet completely assured feeling of self pervaded him, which contained all his earlier, dimly perceived sensations of happiness, only like little bubbles which instantly dissolved in the crystalline flux and luminous clarity of the whole).

20 Consider Hofmannsthal's emphatic defense of the adjective in "Poesie und Leben": "Ich kenne in keinem Kunststil ein Element, das schmählicher verwahrlost wäre als das Eigenschaftswort bei den neueren deutschen sogenannten Dichtern. Es wird gedankenlos hingesetzt oder mit einer absichtlichen Grellmalerei, die alles lähmt (in creative style I know of no element more shamefully neglected by the more recent German so-called poets, than the adjective. It is set down thoughtlessly or with a gaudiness that cripples everything. PI, 264). The polished texture and modulated rhythms in both his and Novalis's prose owe a great deal to the judicious use made of adjectives.

recondite symbolism he employs in *Die Frau ohne Schatten* was, in his own words, designed to bring together the central motifs of his oeuvre: "Vereinigung und Verknüpfung sämtlicher Motive" (A, 218 unification and association of all motifs). The carpet which the young girl spreads before the Kaiser, for instance, is a composite symbol of the unbroken unity of existence, evocatively described in language which owes much to Novalis:

> Das Gewebe war unter seinen Füßen, Blumen gingen in Tiere über, aus den schönen Ranken wanden sich Jäger und Liebende los, Falken schwebten drüber hin wie fliegende Blumen, alles hielt einander umschlungen, eines war ins andere verrankt, das Ganze war maßlos herrlich, eine Kühle stieg aber davon auf, die ihm bis an die Hüften ging. (E, 307)

> (The tapestry lay beneath his feet, flowers blended into animals, huntsmen and lovers slipped out of the lovely tendrils, falcons hovered overhead like flowers in flight, everything fell into an embrace, one being was entwined with another, the whole was marvelous beyond measure, a coolness rose out of it which reached up to his hips).

It is not just the way in which Hofmannsthal weaves together leading motifs but the principles of harmonization and reconciliation operative in the parts of the sentence which strikes one as peculiarly close to Novalis. One might compare this to a passage near the end of "Klingsohrs Märchen" in which "die Erwartung" (the expectation) finds its fulfillment:

> Die Blumen und Bäume wuchsen und grünten mit Macht. Alles schien beseelt. Alles sprach und sang. Fabel grüßt überall alte Bekannte. Die Tieren nahten sich

mit freundlichen Grüßen den erwachten Menschen. Die Pflanzen bewirteten sie mt Früchten und Düften und schmückten sie auf das zierlichste. (SI, 3123)

(The flowers and trees grew and became powerfully verdant. Everything seemed inwardly animate. Everything spoke and sang. Fabel greeted old familiar friends everywhere. The animals approached and awakened people with friendly greetings. The plants waited upon them with fruits and fragrances and adorned them most delicately).

The evocation of the Golden Age, a perfect state of harmony between man and nature, is a comparable linguistic achievement. Like Novalis, Hofmannsthal employs the "Märchen" for its symbolic function and effect in giving form to the complex ideas: the notion of "Tyche" which he saw as an existential force acting in both a divisive and unifying manner; also "das Allomatische," the principle of mutual change, "Die gegenseitige Verwandlung" (A, 21) which is crucial to so many of his works. Like Novalis too, he does not adopt the naïve tone of the children's tale but treats it as a serious literary form.

Nothing in Novalis's writings engaged Hofmannsthal's attention so much as the Fragments, however, for in them he recognized a facility of thought and powers of formulation which were both congenial and stimulating to his creativity. He paid ample tribute to this side of Novalis's genius not just in the two publications by the Bremer Presse of 1922 already mentioned, but more especially in constant reference to and quotations from the Fragments in writing his novel *Andreas*, his numerous essays and in composing his own book of aphorisms and reflections *Das Buch der Freunde* (1922). A survey of all the Fragments which were in some way assimilated into his oeuvre shows that he was drawn particularly to those on poetics, aesthetics, philosophy, religion and the humanities rather than to those on the mathematical or natural sciences.

One of the reflections in the *Buch der Freunde* reads: "Die Fragmente des Novalis können geistige Landschaften vorstellen, in welchen die Zeit besiegt ist" (A, 73 Novalis's Fragments can envisage intellectual landscapes in which time is conquered). The breadth and exploratoriness of thought, the sense of creative boldness in cogitation and also the timeless quality of these ideas is together suggested through Hofmannsthal's imagery.[21] What clearly appealed to him about Novalis's Fragments was their openness of form by means for which a wealth of ideas was generated, in contradistinction to closed forms like the maxim or apothegm which offered a summation of thought. "The aim of all aphorisms," Peter Stern has said, "is not to give a coherent account, but to elicit a response of thought."[22] The nature of a Fragment is to Novalis

---

21 Hofmannsthal confessed to being creatively stimulated by the fragmentary compositions of other artists, another reason why the writings of Novalis held a particular fascination for him" "Künstler lieben vollendete Kunstwerke nicht so sehr we Fragmente, Skizzen, Entwürfe und Studien, weil sie aus solchen am meisten fürs Handwerk lernen können" (Artists do not love complete workd of art so much as fragments, sketches, dreafts and studies, because they can learn most from such as these for their craft A, 92).
22 Joseph Peter Stern, *Lichtenberg: A Doctrine of Scattered Occasions*, London: Thames & Hudson, 1963, p. 112.

a nucleus or germ of thought whose fuller potential meaning is realized in the mind of another; by it the reader is prompted to further speculation. He implies a form designed to engender an abundant fertility of ideas but one which does not itself represent the final fruition. Though the stricter form of aphorism occupies a significant part of Novalis's Fragments, Hofmannsthal was not disposed to make any generic distinctions. He once applied the term "Kristallisationen" (crystallizations) to the Fragments of Novalis (PII, 343), by which term he drew attention to the hard, reductive quality of these "Gedankensplitter" (splinters of thought) as well to their perspicuity.

The degree of empathy and affinity with the aphorist Novalis might, in a negative sense, be attested by the fact that on occasion Hofmannsthal mistakenly attributes to Novalis, as in the much quoted: "Nach einem unglücklichen Krieg müssen Komödien geschrieben werden" (PII, 40 comedies must be written after a disastrous war), or "Gute Gedanken muß man auch von rückwärts anschauen können" (A, 45 one must also be able to view good thoughts in reverse). The authorship of these aphorisms is still in dispute. The aphoristic style Hofmannsthal detected in them, their arresting use of paradox, their bold assertiveness, were sufficient to authenticate them as Novalis's formulations, it seems. The inclination to empathize with a style and a mode of thought is anyhow something characteristic of Hofmannsthal the writer. It is manifest in the very conception of his *Buch der Freunde* which represents an interplay of minds, a discourse of the intellect between the poet and like-minded "friends," historical and contemporary. Novalis was an important member of that select company and the book contains five reflections on him besides three quotations attributed to him.

Something of the intuitive reception and intellectual "Wahlverwandtschaft" (elective affinity) if one lists a number of reflections by them and places them side by side:

1. Symbole sind Mystifikationen, (SII, 560)

1. (Symbols are mystifications).

2. Situationen sind symbolisch; es ist die Schwäche der jetzigen Menschen, daß sie sie analytisch behandeln und dadurch das Zauberische auflösen. (A, 14)

2. (Situations are symbolic; it is a weakness in people today that they treat them analytically and thereby dissolve the element of enchantment).

3. Höchstens kann wahre Poesie einen allegorischen Sinn im großen haben und eine indirekte Wirkung wie Musik usw. (SIII, 572)

3. (True poetry can at best have allegorical meaning in the main and an indirect effect like music etc.).

4. Jede Dichtung ist durch und durch ein Gebilde aus uneigentlichen Ausdrücken. PI, 286)

4. (Every literary work is through and through a composite of non-literal expression).

5. Die Seele des Kunstwerks muß so nackend als möglich auf der Oberfläche liegen. (SIII, 571).

5. (The soul of a work of art must lie as nakedly as possible on the surface).

6. Die Tiefe muß man verstecken. Wo? An der Oberfläche. (A, 17)

6. (One must hide depth. Where? On the surface).

7. Genie ist das synthesierende Prinzip, das Genie macht das Unmögliche möglich – das Mögliche unmöglich – da Unbekannte bekannt – das Bekannte unbekannt etc. (SII, 168)

8. Das Genie bringt Übereinstimmung hervor zwischen der Welt in der es lebt, und der Welt, die in ihm lebt. (A, 79)

9. Alles Leben ist ein überschwenglicher Erneuerungsprozeß. (SII, 556)

10. Das Leben ist restlos Vereinigung des Unvereinbaren. (A, 200)

11. Es gibt Verbindungen aller Art. Eine unendliche Verbindung ist die Ehe. (SIII, 692)

12. Der Sinn der Ehe ist wechselseitige Auflösung und Palingenesie. Wahre Ehe ist darum nur durch den Tod lösbar, ja eigentlich auch durch diesen nicht. (A, 29)

13. Der wahre Leser muß der

7. (Genius is the synthesizing principle; genius makes the impossible possible – the possible impossible – the unknown known – the known unknown etc.).

8. (Genius brings about a congruence between the world in which it lives and the world which lives within it).

9. (All of life is an effusive process of renewal).

10. (Life is total unification of the incompatible).

11. (There are all kinds of unions. One unending union is marriage).

12. (The meaning of marriage is reciprocal dissolution and palingenesis. True marriage can therefore be dissolved only by death, and actually not even by the latter).

13. (The true reader must be the

erweiterte Autor sein. (SII, 470)

14. Ein Buch ist zur großen Hälfte des Lesers Werk. (PIV, 141)

15. Der vollkommene Charakter würde der durchsichtigste – der von selbst verständliche – der unendlich leicht und natürlich scheinende, durchauende bekannte, deshalb unbemerkte, übersehene/und elastiche sein. (SII, 601)

16. Man kann sechsig Jahre alt geworden sein, ohne zu ahnen, was ein Charakter ist. Nichts ist verborgener als die Dinge, die wir beständig im Mund führen. (A, 11)

17. Wir werden die Welt verstehen, wenn wir uns selbst verstehen, weil wir und sie integrante Hälften sind. (SII, 548)

18. Der Mensch wird in der Welt nur das gewahr, was shon in ihm liegt; aber er braucht die Welt, um gewahr zu werden, was in ihm liegt. (A, 9)

extended author).

14. (A book is in larger part the work of the reader).

15. (The most perfect character would be the most transparent – at once comprehensible – one who appears infinitely light and natural, thoroughly known, therefore unnoticed, overlooked and elastic.)

16. (One can have reached the age of sixty without having an inkling as to what a character is. Nothing is more hidden than the things we constantly hold forth about).

17. (We shall understand the world when we understand ourselves, since we and it are integrant parts).

18. (Man only perceives in the world that which is already within him; but he needs the world in order to perceive what lies within him).

19. Menschheit ist eine humoristische Rolle. (SII, 437)	19. (Humanity is a humorous role).
20. Menschen in Bezug auf Menschen sind bloß immer komisch. (A, 15)	20. (Human beings in relation to other human beings are always simply comical).

The odd number are sayings by Novalis, the even by Hofmannsthal. This selection, which might well be extended, shows that Hofmannsthal the aphorist was equally drawn to philosophical topics of the broadest scope (e. g. genius, character, humanity, self and world) though the body of his aphorisms is small compared to that of Novalis. There is in Hofmannsthal's thought a quality of reverential awe, a nimbus of mystification which is not unlike Novalis and yet something apart. The suggestive use of paradox, chiasmus, analogue and figurative means, though devices native to aphoristic style, reveal certain comparable features between them. However, the characteristic mode of Novalis's thinking in opposites or contrasts through a progressive chain of association, which cannot fully be presented by these succincter examples, is not Hofmannsthal's method. The openness of the typical Novalis Fragment finds its correspondence in Hofmannsthal's more speculative approach. The latter broaches the topic more tentatively (as in nos. 2, 12, 16) stating a proposition more commonly than making an assertion. In Novalis there is a distinctive urgency of thought, an audacity and impatience of the will to open new frontiers to ideas. In Hofmannsthal one detects a greater love of the *aperçu* – a trait also reflected in the numerous quotations from French writers in the collection. The infectious exuberance of no. 9 or the mystic idealism of 11 and 17 find their correspondence in Hofmannsthal's more meditative tone. If one compares nos. 11 and 12 on the subject of marriage, one notes in Novalis's formulation the typical aspiring movement of the mind from the familiar premise to transcendent idea. In Hofmannsthal (no. 12) the recondite opening reflection about mutual transformation and rebirth is quite differently qualified in the second sentence. The idea of transcendence beyond death is given, but the appended clause ("ja, eigntlich auch durch diesen nicht") is discreetly cautious and the final note is one of suspended speculation.

For Novalis "Dichten" (creative writing) and "Denken" (thinking) are such closely interfused activities (what he called willkürlicher, tätiger, produktiver Gebrauch unserer Organe") (SIII, 563 willful, active productive use of our organs), that they become for him identical. The intuitive nature of his thought, which never excluded imagination and feeling, was something to which Hofmannsthal could perfectly relate. Indeed he perceived an affinity between Novalis's associative intuition as to the dualism of body and mind to that of Tolstoy and Dostoevsky (A, 63). For such reasons as these Novalis figures ever more prominently in the later essays as a writer could be quoted alongside Goethe and Kleist, Schiller or Hölderlin (PIV, 144, 147) as a fixed point of reference, as one from whom one can learn and who continues to exercise an influence within German culture.

The fragmentary notes which comprise much of the unfinished novel *Andreas oder die Vereinigten* (Andreas or the United) again reflect the central significance of Novalis as a mainstay of thought on form and content, a master of formulation whose innovative intellect constantly helps him to crystallize ideas. It is not for nothing that Hofmannsthal relates the key concept of "Vereinigung" (unification) – an idea which lies at the heart of Novalis as poet and thinker – to his "Poetik des Übels" (SIII, 389 Poetics of Evil), that complex Fragment in which the divisive power of evil is explored and its demise through "Verbindung" (combination) is philosophically proposed. Hofmannsthal's own concept of "das Allomatische," the principle of mutual transformation as one important means of attaining wholeness, though not exclusively indebted to Novalis, nonetheless shows an affinity with his idealistic thought.

The reception of Novalis by Hofmannsthal which we have surveyed under three principal aspects, the poet's sense of identity, the role of symbolic language and the importance of the Fragment, allows one to draw a number of inferences. Hofmannsthal did not maintain the same relationship to Novalis from his early beginnings to maturity. A change from unconscious impressionability and assimilation to a much more aware philosophical response is to be see in the later Hofmannsthal. He was constantly evolving as a writer and as his circle of interests widened, so his attitudes were modified or revised. In respect of his susceptibility to literary influence, he is perhaps the most chameleon-like writer since Goethe. Michael Hamburger has well described this trait in him:

> Hofmannsthal war einer der Dichter, die auf Umwegen zu sich selber zurückkehren, mit Mitteln bewaffnet, die ihre Organe geworden sind: zu den Umwegen gehörten

die Werke anderer Menschen, die Hofmannsthal lesend erlebte, drum auch wie alles Erlebte in das eigene Werk aufnahm.[23]

(Hofmannsthal was one of those poets who return to themselves by circuitous paths, armed with resources which have become their organs: to these circuitous paths belonged the works of others whom Hofmannsthal experienced in his reading and thus, like all other experience, absorbed into his own work).

Hofmannsthal not only absorbed, but was in part altered by each new literary encounter or intellectual contact which arrested his mind. So it was in the case of his reception of Novalis. The interest in another mind never meant simple assimilation of an extraneous source but involved a process of transformation through the creative act. Hofmannsthal alters what he treats, refashioning his material according to need. The material thus becomes his own and blends into the new form. Theodor Heuss in his commemorative speech of July 3, 1965 put the issue conclusively and memorably:

> Ist Hofmannsthal ein Wanderer durch Geschichte und Geschichten, der fremde Motive bedarf? So its es nicht: er verfügt und verwandelt, er besitzt und gestaltet.[24]

(Is Hofmannsthal a wanderer through history and histories, who has need of extraneous motifs? Not so: he disposes and transforms, he possesses and forms).

---

23 Michael Hamburger, "Hofmannsthals Bibliothek: Ein Bericht," Euph 55, 1961, p. 76.
24 Theodor Heuss, *Hugo von Hofmannsthal: Eine Rede*, Tübingen: Leins, 1954, p. 17.

W. B. Yeats and Hofmannsthal as Exponents of Lyrical Drama*

Gnug, den Poeten bindet keine Zeit
—Goethe Faust II

Wir sind deine Flügel, O Zeit, dich wir wir nicht die tragende Klaue!
Oder verlangst du so viel: Flügel und Klaue zugleich?
—Hugo von Hofmannsthal

The final decade of the nineteenth century, in which literary historians are wont to see the genesis of "modern literature," was equally a time of great creative ferment and experiment on the stage where, in the wake of Wagner's "Gesamtkunstwerk," new dramatic theories and forms vied for public attention. The contest between the two dominant aesthetic trends of that period, Naturalism and Symbolism proved, one may claim, both beneficial and fruitful, for it helped to stimulate creativity

---

* Textual reference to W. B. Yeats's works are to the following editions with the abbreviations listed:
Au   *Autobiographies*, London, 1955
E & I   *Essays and Introductions*, London 1961
L   *Letters*, edited by Allan Wade, London 1954
M   *Mythologies*, London 1959
Me   *Memoirs*, London 1972
P   *Collected Poems*, Second ed., with later poems added, London 1940
Pl   *Collected Plays*, Second ed. with additional Plays, London 1952.

and innovation. Making due allowance for the levelling force of generalization, we can place in one camp the dramatists Ibsen, Chekhov, Hauptmann and Schnitzler as representative of the Naturalist persuasion, and in the other Maeterlinck, Yeats, Hofmannsthal and Claudel, who all looked to a Symbolist aesthetic as their guiding star. Leaving aside the social satirists Shaw and Wedekind, who took up a more individualist polemical stance, the polarized debate concerning the nature of drama and its appropriate form on the contemporary stage were fervently pursued between these two opposing positions; the one radical in its demands for realism and precise social-historical awareness, the other no less emphatic in its call for inner truth of expression through beauty of language and form. While Naturalism claimed originality by virtue of its scientific approach, by its choice of raw subject-matter and real-life idiomatic Symbolism zealously restored myth and archetype, and revitalized the latent powers of poetic tradition. Each movement saw itself in the light of innovation, as a new way forward in the art of theater. Something of the complexity surrounding the on-going debate of the 1890'a is captured by Chekhov in Act One of *The Seagull*, where Treplev's so-called 'decadent' allegorical play evokes among its first hearers a mixture of estrangement, ridicule, and genuine emotion. The failed experiment is, of course, shown as incomplete since it is interrupted, yet the suggestion remains that the intimacy and empathy demanded by the new drama involves a more refined response and that the lyrical play will need to fight for recognition in a hostile world of sober realism.

The lyrical drama developed by Yeats and Hofmannsthal in that decade and later, bears the stamp of its age as part of the European Symbolist movement and may be seen, in the first instance, as a distinctive response to the challenge presented by the historical moment. An instinctive antagonism to the 'materialists' of the age, to scientific rationalism, to 'that now old and much respected dogmatist, the Spirit of the Age, as the young Yeats called it,[1] found a ready target in the plays of the Naturalists. The early Yeats and Hofmannsthal were, quite independently, working towards a similar dramatic goal, beguiled and inspired by the same siren voices pressing for the refinement of style, musicality and formal beauty: Baudelaire, Malarmé, Pater, Maeterlinck, Wilde. Both Yeats and Hofmannsthal were essentially lyric poets *ab initio* and they evolved a subtle new dramatic medium which in conception, language and form was to stand as an alternative to the plays then being produced by an Ibsen or a Hauptmann. Yeats recalled hearing *The Doll's House* described as "a series of conversations terminated by an accident," and added that he "resented being invited to admire dialogue so close to modern educated speech that music and style were impossible" (Au 279). "Music and style" for Yeats and for Hofmannsthal remained essential and permanent prerequisites for good writing. To these should be added the element of rhythm which Hofmannsthal pronounced "das Ausschlaggebende" (the decisive element) in good style, indeed, it represented for him "der Hebel

---

[1] p. 3 Introduction to *Fairy and Folk Tales of the Irish Peasantry*, edited by W. B. Yeats, The Scott Library, London: Scott, 1888, p. IX.

aller Wirkung" (PI 264 the fulcrum of all expressiveness), for the secret of rhythm lay not merely in the poets' choice of words and their arrangement but more especially in the sensitive use of the adjective.[2] Hofmannsthal too was critical of what he saw as Ibsen's "nordic-protestant rigidity and want of affability" which prevented him from creating comedy out of his dramatic subjects (A. 63). In writing a critical study of "Die Menschen in Ibsens Dramen" (1893 "The People in Ibsen's Drama") he finds that the playwright's figures are basically derived from a single principle type, a sharply perceived modern type, who is animated by the spirit of the author, Hofmannsthal elaborates:

> Alle diese Menschen leben ein schattenhaftes Leben; sie erleben fast keine Taten und Dinge, fast ausschließliche Gedanken, Stimmungen und Verstimmungen. Sie wollen wenig, sie tun fast nichts. Sie denken übers Denken, fühlen sich fühlen und treiben Autopsychologie (PI, 88)

> (All these people live a shadowy life, they experience almost no deeds or things, but almost exclusively thoughts, moods and aggravations. They want little, they do almost nothing. They think about thinking, feel their feelings and engage in auto-psychology.)

As Hofmannsthal was just nineteen when he wrote this critique and had only just begun to turn his hand to dramatic subjects, we may not find it so surprising that what he is describing reveals more about his own methods than Ibsen's. The young Hofmannsthal is a discriminating critic, yet the impressionist in

---

2 p. 33 "Poesie und Leben" (PI, 264-265).

him is chameleon-like; too ready with empathy, too keen in his search for an artistic identity, to cut out the self while enquiring into another (and admired) creative intelligence. The tribute of admiration for the older dramatist which Hofmannsthal is conveying, will not be denied; it is offered implicitly in the final sentence through the tell-tale mirror-image of narcissism:

> Aber man geht durch die reiche und schweigende Seele eines wunderbaren Menschen, mit Mondlicht, phantastischen Schatten und wanderndem Wind und schwarzen Seen, stillen Spiegeln, in denen man sich selbst erkennt gigantisch vergrößert und unheimlich schön verwandelt. (PI, 98)

> (but one moves through the rich and speechless soul of a marvelous human being, through moonlight, fantastic mirrors in which one recognizes oneself, gigantically enlarged and transformed by wondrous beauty.)

Hofmannsthal's rejection of Naturalism as a literary movement was not unqualified or dogmatic, neither did it obscure from him the artistic merits of Ibsen or Hauptmann. (The significant influence of Georg Büchner on Hofmannsthal is added proof of his receptivity to another form of Naturalism). He was also on the best of terms with Hauptmann, as the recently published record of their literary relations clearly shows, recognizing him as 'a true poet' and maintaining an enduring, if not uncritical, interest in his work.[3] Hofmannsthal's objections to Naturalism were of a more fundamental kind and directed at what he perceived as a mistaken aesthetic. While Yeats declared that he "did

---
3 HB Heft 37/38, 1988, p. 14.

not care for mere reality" (Au 83) and that "realism is created for the common people and was always their peculiar delight" (E & I 227), Hofmannsthal recorded in his *Book of Friends*:

> Naturalismus entfernt sich von der Natur, weil er, um die Oberfläche nachzumachen, das innere Beziehungsreiche, das eigentliche Mysterium der Natur, vernachläßigen muß. (A 81)

(Naturalism is a departure from nature because, in order to copy the surface, it must needs neglect the wealth of internal relationships, the essential mystery of nature.)

The profound rejection of a realism of surface features was fully shared by Yeats, who continually stressed the importance of "the mystical life" and saw himself as part of that "greater renaissance" of the revolt of the soul against the intellect (L 211). The reinstatement of mystery, the discovery of the drama of the soul and the mysticism of common experience became the central tenets of the new lyrical drama and were eloquently formulated in Maeterlinck's book *The Treasure of the Humble* (1897) which repudiated all the manifestos of the Naturalists. While Yeats had reservations about Maeterlinck's actual dramatic achievement, he acknowledged his immense value "as a force helping people to understand the more ideal drama" (L 255). It will therefore be my purpose to define and evaluate the nature of this so-called ideal drama as developed by Yeats and Hofmannsthal, and to assess its symbolism in terms of its temporal application and meaning.

Despite cultural and formative differences in their backgrounds, Yeats and Hofmannsthal have been seen (notably by T. S.

Eliot and Michael Hamburger) as kindred spirits, fashioning from the treasure-house of tradition a whole range of similar subjects with often surprisingly comparable results.[4] Their writings reveal so many points of contact as common ground might provide something in the nature of an "abstract profile" for this unusual convergence of two creative minds. We note in both: a deep commitment to cultural tradition, the preeminent significance they attach to form; to the importance of myth, symbol and dream, an interest in the esoteric, the mystical and the spiritual; the insistence on beauty, on style, on musicality in language; the role of the mask and the persona, the fostering of aristocratic values; the cultivation of a national consciousness of identity through literature and theater.[5] To this might be added that both poets were translators of the tragedy of Oedipus, both constantly drew on the Greek myths for inspiration and were instinctively drawn to the topos of Leda and the Swan. They also reserved a special status for one recurring person who acquires something like mythical significance. Yeats has his Chuchulain, the heroic lover, "the wild will of man" (PI 261), Hofmannsthal has his "Abenteurer";

---

4 Michael Hamburger, Introduction to Hugo von Hofmannsthal, *Poems and Verse Plays*, London: Routledge & Paul, 1961, p. LVI and passim. Also Joan K. Renz, *Yeats and the Germans: A Dramatic Kinship Twice Removed*, Ann Arbor MI: UMI, 1980 [diss. University of Connecticut 1979], chap 3.

5 Such enumeration of shared literary allegiances might be extended to include the many, more specific, figures and ideas like Plato, Goethe, Nietzsche, Balzac, Shelley or Browning; yet its function here is primarily to show the firm outline of a far-reaching intellectual affinity which certainly deserves wider exploration.

"Der Abenteurer, jener die umfassende, umarmende Geist – in die Sphäre des Lebens gefallen: der Zeit und den verändernden Gewalten ausgeliefert" (A, 221 The adventurer, that spirit which encompasses, embraces a totality – fallen into the sphere of life at the mercy of time and the powers of change).

There is also close agreement between the two poets in their understanding of symbolism. A metaphoric style is for both the native element of poetry, and each employs his own in a wholly natural, unconstrained manner. On the nature of metaphoric diction, Hofmannsthal pronounced: "vielmehr ist der uneigentliche, der bildliche Ausdruck Kern und Wesen aller Poesie" (Pl. 286 rather, non-specific, figurative expression is the very core and essence of all poetry). Yeats preferred to speak of "symbolic writing"; since for him the symbol was an intensified metaphor "because metaphors are not profound enough to be moving, when they are not symbols, and when they are symbols they are the most perfect of all, because the more subtle, outside of pure sound, and through them one can best find out what symbols are" (E & I, 156). He stressed the elements of "suggestion" and "evocation" in symbolism, and tried to distinguish between "emotional symbols" and "intellectual symbols," though he conceded that emotions might be mingled with ideas. Yeats also believed the symbol had the power to invoke meanings, as he wrote in his Journal: "Every symbol is an invocation which produces its equivalent expression in all worlds" (Me, 166). He saw no place for "the invention of the will" (i.e. mere mechanical contrivance) in serious poetry, but strongly advocated the "return to imagination" and sensuous rhythm which alone could engender the enduring symbol:

> We would seek out those wavering, meditative, organic rhythms, which are the embodiment of the imagination, that neither desires nor hates, because it has done with time, and only wishes to gaze upon some reality, some beauty. (E & I, 163)

This stress on intuitive perception, accords with Hofmannsthal's succinct and telling definition of the symbol as "das sinnliche Bild für geistige Wahrheit, die der Ratio unerreichbar ist" (PIV, 49) (the same sensuous image of spiritual truth which is inaccessible into pure reason). Yeats once spoke of "open symbolism" (Me, 283) in an art review, to intimate something of the breadth of suggestiveness a symbol may contain. He was peculiarly sensitive to the many shades of clarity or preciseness in the use of symbol, as his essay on "The Philosophy of Shelley's Poetry" shows. He was no less alive to the obscurity of allusion or reference in his own more personal symbolism than he was to Shelley or Blake.[6] His more particular interest in what he termed "ancient symbolism" (like Water, Fire, the Moon, the Sun, the Star, the Tower, the Dancer, which are archetypal or the property of tradition) is closely tied to his poetic mission as the reviver of national myth and legend. The firm connection between ancient and modern is repeatedly stated: "we Irish poets, modern men

---

6 In a letter to Elizabeth C. Yeats (autumn 1920) Yeats explicates the symbolism of *The Unicorn from the Stars* in these terms: "the truth is that it is a private symbol belonging to my mystical order and nobody knows what it comes from. It is the soul" (L, 662).

also, reject every folk art that does not go back to Olympus" (E & I, 513) he writes in an introduction to his work. Or again: "We did not look forward or look outward, we left that to the prose writers; we looked back" (E & I, 495). Hofmannsthal too was profoundly aware that nothing could bind past and present more meaningfully than the poetic symbol. As an Austrian poet, he felt the pull of tradition more powerfully than most and, like Years, was acutely conscious of the poet's role as mediator of a nation's past, as a spokesman of tradition. In his essay "Österreich im Spiegel seiner Dichtung" ("Austria in the Mirror of its Poetry") he asserted that "Das Alte und das Neue ist nebeneinander da, ist wirklich bei uns ein bißchen mehr als anderswo" (PIII, 341 the old and the new is present side by side, it is truly a little more present amongst us than elsewhere). Hofmannsthal's tireless dedication to the revival of traditional forms of theater, whether Attic tragedy, medieval or baroque drama, Italian or French comedy, is a manifest attempt to bring past and present together by the power of symbolism. For without the binding and communicative aura of the symbol, tradition remains a dead letter, Hofmannsthal was especially intent upon revitalizing the *theatrum mundi* in Austria, where it had survived longest, and referred to it as "a mystery or a great allegory" which had not yet lost its power (A. 210). He believed that he had only just managed to rescue the torch of tradition from extinction by blending older and modern features, not just in his form, but in all his other works too, (A, 202).

Looking back across his literary career, the mature Yeats wrote in 1937: "I have never said clearly that I condemn all that is not tradition" (E & I, viii), and in the same year he stated vehemently: "I hated and still hate with an ever-growing hatred the literature of the point of view" (E & I, 511). The passionately held conviction that literature bears within its stream the "deposits" of ancient subject-matter, mythologies, archetypes and symbols, to which the poet gives ever renewed form, is one Hofmannsthal shared, for he speaks of the poet not as the servant of time but as "der Überwinder der Zeit" (II, 257 the conqueror of time). In his essay of 1907, "Der Dichter in dieser Zeit" ("The Poet in our Time"), he questions the very possibility of any tangible concept of "the present" and proposes instead the purely evocative notion "Atmosphäre unserer Zeit" (PII, 233 The atmosphere of our times). As a traditionalist he would also have concurred with Yeats's condemnation of tendentious or partisan writing which narrowly addresses the issues of the day. Even though the mythical subject of Yeats's first play might seem rather remote from the concerns of his contemporary society, the public outcry surrounding *The Countess Cathleen* (1892) on the occasion proved the reverse. Yeats wrote of the affair in retrospect: "In using what I considered traditional symbols I forgot that in Ireland they are not symbols but realities" (Au, 416). It is an instance of symbolism falling prey to the prejudices of the times. Even though it had not been written "in the manner of Ibsen, in the manner of the moment" (Au, 417) the symbolic play could and did become the battle-ground for a specific religious and political controversy.[7]

---

[7] For Yeats's own account of the historical circumstances surrounding the event, one needs to consult his notes in an early edition, such as

If Yeats's championing of the new poetic drama is accompanied by an intermittent aggressiveness and stridency in tone, Hofmannsthal's advocacy tends to assume a more persuasive eloquence. In his essay of 1903 "Die Bühne als Traumbild' ("The Stage as Dream Image") he employs allusive metaphoric language rather than hard argument to conjure up a picture of the stage as a place of mystery and dream-like atmosphere. Nonetheless a number of definite ideas are proposed; in the first place, the aim in staging must be "Ein Bild schaffen, auf dem nicht Fußbreit ohne Bedeutung ist" (PII, 63 to create an image, in which not the smallest space is without significance). The stage must not represent rigid separation but show the connectedness of all things, a fluidity of relationships; stage props must be strongly evocative, atmospheric, full of enchantment. The images on stage should be of exceptional simplicity, not copied from real life, but such as to stimulate in us a more vivid inner vision of a dream. These ideas are in close agreement with Yeats's call for a bare stage with the minimum of suggested detail, as he wrote in a letter of 1897: "My own theory of poetical or legendary drama is that it should have no realistic or elaborate, but only a symbolic or decorative setting." (L, 280). He also looked for settings which drew little visual attention but appealed to the imagination, preferring an "austere and monotonous beauty" which did not divert attention

---

The Land of Hearts Desire, The Countess Cathleen, Benn's Essex Library, London: Benn, 1929, pp. 145-156. He calls his subject "one of the supreme parables of the world," yet is equally aware that even the audiences of the Abbey Theatre "are almost ignorant of Irish mythology."

from the spoken word (L. 209). The reference to time in the settings of Yeats's plays are generally open and unspecific. *The Countess Cathleen* is set "in old times," *The Land of Heart's Desire* "in a remote time," the Chuchulain plays in a legendary Ireland; *Cathleen ni Houlihan* and *The Dreaming of Bones* alone are set in the specific revolutionary years of Irish history, 1798 and 1916 respectively, yet as clearly patriotic allegories, their style consistently functions at the level of metaphor and encourages a timeless effect. Hofmannsthal's settings more often involve references to historical epochs, but again only for evocative, atmospheric purposes: the later Renaissance in *Gestern (Yesterday)* and *Der Tod des Tizian (The Death of Titian)* the 1820's for *Der Tor und der Tod (Death and the Fool)* mid-18th-century Venice for *Der Abenteurer und die Sangerin (The Adventurer and the Singer)* Byzantium for *Der Kaiser und die Hexe (The Emperor and the Witch)*, yet another cultural symbol he shared with Yeats. Neither makes much of the historical context for other than poetic ends.

The object of lyrical drama is not action but expressive representation, revelation, the unfolding of the inner life; it lays stress on evocativeness, not on the logic of causation. As Peter Szondi has succinctly formulated: "Lyrisches Drama ist nicht dialogisierte Lyrik, sondern imaginäres Theater" (lyrical drama is not dialogized poetry, but theater of the mind).[8] Hofmannsthal

---

[8] Peter Szondi, *Das lyrische Drama des Fin de Siècle*, Frankfurt am Main: Suhrkamp, 1975, p. 59. See also James W. Flannery, W. B. Yeats and the Idea of a Theater, New Haven London: Yale University Press, 1976, especially chapter 5 "A Dramatist in Search of a Theatrical Form."

distrusted what he called "zweckvolles Gepräch" (purposeful dialogue) as a vehicle for drama. He claimed: "Die Dialektik dringt das Ich aus der Existenz. Ich behaupte ein Dichter hat die Wahl, Reden zu schaffen, oder Gestalten" (PIV, 458 Dialectics thrust the ego out of existence. I maintain that a poet has the choice of creating either speeches or characters). The *drama statique* evolved by Maeterlinck created an illusion of suspended time; it showed figures who are passive in their dreamlike existence, who yield to powers beyond their control.[9] The poet's choice of a mythical setting was designed to evoke a universal, timeless symbol. Following Maeterlinck, Yeats wrote of his own "rejection of all needless movement" (E & I, 528): "I wanted to get rid of irrelevant movement – the stage must become still that words might keep all their vividness" (E & I, 527). The shift of interest from dramatic action to an involvement in atmosphere, in an inward intensity of experience, threw the weight of emphasis on to the expressiveness of language. Raymond Williams's nice formulation of Yeats's aim is worth recalling: "a realized drama which would have the status of poetry, a rich and penetrating form which should reveal, not character, but those deeper forces of which character is merely a lineament."[10] Hofmannsthal became aware in retrospect of how much the "lyrical subject" naturally tended to the condition of music, and that he was the predestined librettist. As he wrote in

---

9 Maurice Maeterlinck, *Treasure of the Humble*, translated by Alfred Sutro, London: Allen, 1924, pp. 106-107.
10 Raymond Williams, *Drama from Ibsen to Eliot*, Harmondsworth: Penguin, 1964, p. 230.

his essay "Die ägyptische Helena" (1928 "The Egyptian Helen"): "schon meine ersten Dramen hatten bewußt nach Musik verlangt, und das Wort 'lyrisch' deute dies nur ungenau an" (PIV, 441 my very first dramas had unconsciously been calling for music, and the word 'lyrical' only vaguely hints at this). The lyrical drama is, in effect, a potential libretto.[11]

The claim has been made that Hofmannsthal's early and rapid development from writing dramatic lyrics to writing lyrical dramas, was particularly influenced by his interest in the French Symbolists. In fact, unlike the French Symbolists, who opted for exotic and arcane subjects with an unworldly, artificial beauty, Hofmannsthal introduces a profoundly ethical accentuation into even his earliest plays.[12] The argument for an organic progression and growth in stature from his lyrical beginning to his mature dramatic works is, to my mind, persuasive, while it also does away with the tired fiction of an *oeuvre* divided in two by a crisis of language. Hofmannsthal remained a poet to the last, even in his later, more realistic comedies. He, like Yeats, was first attracted to the form of the dramatic "Rollengedicht" (poems which speak through a generic figure or persona). This form, which is especially indebted to Browning's dramatic monologues, might be described as the enactment of a dramatic idea within a single consciousness.

---

11 Hofmannsthal explicitly refers to lyrical dramas as opera in a letter to his publisher S. Fischer, February 25, 1922, "die lyrischen Dramen (alias Opern)," in H/Almanach, p. 134.
12 Cf. Thomas Kovach, *Hofmannsthal and Symbolism: Art and Life in the Work of a Modern Poet*, New York Berne Frankfurt am Main: Lang, 1985.

The adopted persona acquires for Yeats the function of a mask or anti-self, basically defined as "a kind of private mythology in which the individual struggles to become that which is most unlike itself."[13] Hofmannsthal's poetic method may also be said to involve the use of masks, for his protean imagination and capacity for empathizing with "Gestalten" (figures) leads to similar results. In one way or another the mask becomes an objective correlative of the poet's self, even though it is alien or antithetical. Yeats wrote in *Per Amica Silentia Lunae* "The other self, the anti-self or the antithetical self, as one may choose to name it, comes but to those who are no longer deceived, whose passion is reality" (M, 331). The Mask is experienced as an active counter-force, as a stern challenge which comes to the poet. There is a striking parallel to be drawn between Hofmannsthal's application of the idea of "Tyche" and Yeats's doctrine of the Mask. Hofmannsthal speaks of "Tyche" (in mythology the goddess Fortuna) as "ein unerträglicher Dämon" (an unendurable daimon) and defines it as "Die Welt, die das Individuum von sich entfernen will, um es zu sich zu bringen" (A, 222 the world that wishes to ward off the individual so as to bring him to self-awareness).[14] It is remarkable that Yeats

---

13 John Unterecker, *A Reader's Guide to William Butler Yeats*, London: Thames & Hudson, 1959, p. 16. For the most discriminating account of the doctrine of the mask cf. Richard Ellmann, op. cit., pp 171-176. The most pertinent passages on the mask in Yeats may be found in *Per Amica Silentia Lunae* in *Mythologies*, pp. 325-366.

14 See also "Kreuzwege" in Age of Innocence "Stationen einer Entwicklung" (Stages in a Development) (Pl, 134) where Hofmannsthal speaks of the original Greek meaning of "Tyche" as "das Zufällig-Zugefallene" (the accidental which occurs by chance).

also refers to the antagonistic powers of trial and temptation by the term "daimon," though he does so with rather more mystical connotation than Hofmannsthal: "Each Daimon is drawn to whatever man or, if its nature is more general, to whatever nation it most differs from, and shapes into its own image the antithetical dream of man or nation" (M, 362). For both poets these antipodal mechanisms of self-distancing and self-discovery, alienation and insight, the whole problem of the poet's exploration of the self through masks, are very much shared preoccupations; and the symbols chosen to embody this dialectic take the form of a series of personae in their lyrical dramas. Hofmannsthal offers some searching observations on the workings of the poetic imagination in the year 1901, soon after he had published the last of his lyrical dramas. His method of writing always began, as he explained, with a vaguely conceived situation or atmosphere (be it heroic, patriarchal, middle-class, idyllic), which was nonetheless distinctive and unlike any other form. From this a figure would gradually emerge with its own gesture and tone. The final stage for the poet is then unified understanding or vision: "Diese präzise Vision läßt sich dann verstehen. Sie ist immer Symbol, wie alles im Leben, wenn man es in einem günstigen Augenblick tief genug erblickt" (Br. I, 337 The precise vision can then be understood. It is always a symbol, like everything in life, if one perceives it profoundly enough at a favorable moment). The importance attributed to the dramatic figure, not as an individualized character but as the articulation of an idea, the carrier of symbolic meaning, is crucial. The imagined figure always precedes the idea. The emphasis on symbolic roles and their constellation, rather than on conflicts produced by a dramatic action, creates dream-like stasis in which the poetry of the single voice is given space to unfold.[15] This tendency is developed to the fullest extent in Hofmannsthal's *Das kleine Welttheater* (1897 *The Small World Theater*) the least dramatic or theatrical of his early playlets. In dramatic terms it is little more than a succession of voices or anonymous "Gestalten" that move onto the stage by turn and speak in soliloquy, each having its own contrastive rhythm and verse. Hofmannsthal's opening stage direction requires the prominent central positioning of a bridge. The bridge appears symbolic of the idea of communication or mediation, as it intimates the characteristic Hofmannsthalian concept of "Bezüge"; the intangible "links" or subtle relationships between the figures introduced and also between them and the world. Each of them speaks in either direct or figurative terms of the interdependence of men's destinies, the mysterious connectedness of human lives. First one hears the Poet as he muses on the inner life of strangers which fascinate him by their alluring otherness:

---

15 "Bidlicher Ausdruck," Pl, 286: "Die Handlungen, die Gestalten sind niochts anderes, sofern man das Wort nur recht versteht: Gleichnisse aus vielen Gleichnissen zusammengesetzt. Mit der Sprache ist es nicht anders, nur sin des unter den Redened die Dichter allein, die sich des Gleichnishaften der Sprache unaufhörlich bewußt bleiben" ("Actions" and "figures" are nothing else, if the word is properly understood than the allegories made up of many allegories. It is no different with language, yet among those who use speech, it is the poets alone who remain constantly aware of the allegorical nature of language.)

Gestalten! Und sie unterreden sich.
O wüßt ich nur davon! Ein Schicksal ist,
Und irgenwie bin ich dareinverwebt. (GLD, 374)

(Strange figures! They discourse together,
Oh, if I only knew the sense! It is a fate,
And somehow I am interwoven with it.)

The last lines of his speech reiterate this idea of worldly communion, of the Poet bound ineluctably to his role as participant in all human life; but now it is his art "jenes künstliche Gebild" (that work of artifice) which mediates for others that strange heavy sense of involvement in destinies not their own. What Hofmannsthal is depicting is the inception of moral consciousness:

O wüßt ich mehr von diesen Abenteuern,
Denn irgendwie bin ich dareinverwebt
Und weiß nicht, wo sich Traum und Leben spalten
(GLD, 377)

(Oh would that I knew more of these adventures,
For somehow I am interwoven with them,
And do not know where dream and life divide.)

The Gardener also points to the essential oneness of "dies bunte Leben" ("bunt" meaning both diverse and colorful) by the same figure of speech as he contemplates his world of plant life (a metaphor of social existence):

So verwoben sind die Gaben
Des Lebens hier; mir winkt aus jedem Beet
Mehr als ein Mund wie Wunden oder Flammen
Mit schattenhaft durchsichtiger Gebärde,
Und Kindlichkeit und Majestät mitsammen. (GLD, 379)

> (The gifts of life are here so wondrously
> Entwined: from every bed of flowers there beckons
> To me more than one mouth, like would or flame,
> With shadowy, transparent gesture,
> Where childlikeness and majesty conjoin.)

The dreamy Young Gentleman (very much a period figure) then uses a variant of this metaphor of being caught in the toils of other human destinies:

> Ich weiß, ich bin zu jung, und kann die vielerlei
> Geschicke nicht verstehn; vielmehr sie kommen mir
> Wie Netze und Fußangeln vor, in die der Mensch
> Hineingerät und fallend sich verfängt (GLD, 379)

> (I know I am too young and cannot comprehend
> These divers destinies; indeed they seem to me
> like nets and snares into which people stumble
> And falling, get entangled.)

The Hofmannsthalian idea that human lives even in their solitude, are linked like those of the Stranger and the Girl, by the very hope, yearning or memory which fills that solitude, finds expression through the isolated vice of each figure. Finally, through the mouth of the Servant, we are introduced to the last, climactic figure, the Madman in him the dominant motif of a shared human destiny finds distorted expression, for his frenzied life has been insatiable pleasure and conquest His significance as "eine Form der erreichten Vollkommenheit" (A, 223 a form of achieved perfection), in Hofmannsthal's own words, must appear enigmatic. Yet there is something impressive about his passionate self-surrender to a manic quest for the innermost secrets of life:

"einen unerhörten Weg zu suchen/In den Kern des Lebens" (GLD, 389 to seek an unheard of path into the core of life). Only lyrical drama with its evocative registers and "open symbolism" can presume to capture the symbolic complexity of such a visionary figure.[16] He is represented as one who is in the grip of his daimon: "die rätselhafte Gottheit" (GLD, 389 the enigmatic deity) a man who bears within him a multiple destiny: "zehntausendmal das Schicksal von zehntausend Bergen" (GLD, 393 ten thousand times the destiny of ten thousand mountains) – a destiny which impels him to the brink of self-destruction. The Madman shows up a weakness in Hofmannsthal to overload figures with meaning; a weakness which persists to his very last symbolic drama, *Der Turm* (*The Tower*).

It is as much a fallacy to look for self-portraits in these early dramatic figures of Hofmannsthal's, as it is to look for them in Yeats's. It would be much nearer the truth to see them as searching explorations of alien aspects of the self the equivalent of Yeats's *Masks*. Unlike Hofmannsthal, Yeats put theoretical masks on many of his characters to stylize them and accentuate their symbolic role. Both poets consistently "looked back" to tradition, choosing for their plays figures with a universal symbolism derived from an aristocratic, hierarchic order, whose very names are their meaning: the Emperor, the King, the Beggar, the Blind

---

16 Hofmannsthal no more than hinted at the complex meaning vested in the Madman in a late note: "Das ich als Spiegel des Ganzen aber mehr als Spiegel: der Wahnsinnige" (A, 228 The Ego as the mirror of the whole, but more than the mirror: the Madman).

Man, the Wise Man, the Fool etc. These titles convey a pre-established stateliness and dignity into their roles, even in a modern context. The modern poet could call upon the symbolic power that is already vested in their traditional functions and connotations. Thus Hofmannsthal was able to draw on medieval mystery and miracle plays to create his own *Everyman* and *The Salzburg Great World Theater*, while Yeats turned to Irish myth and folklore as the basis for his heroic plays on Chuchulain or to the Japanese Noh theater for his *Four Plays for Dancers*. Both treated the dramatic figure as a symbolic mask and neither could forget that, as Yeats wrote in 1899, "the theater began in ritual and it cannot come to its greatness again without recalling words to their ancient sovereignty" (E & I, 170).

Of course, by no means all of these plays of the pre-war period were in the heroic mould. Unable to escape the influence of his admired fellow-countryman Synge, Yeats frequently drew upon the Irish peasantry for his figures and even allowed a vernacular strain to enter his poetic diction. Hofmannsthal too opens his theatrical career by depicting characters who clearly belong to the *fin-de-siècle*, and who, as symbols of the time, reflect its tone as well as its defects and moral frailties: there is Andrea, the hedonistic impressionist who wantonly plays with fidelity until it is avenged on him; Claudio, the decadent aesthete whom Death calls a "Fool" since he has chosen to experience life through art; Elis, the deluded seeker for a chimerical, unearthly love; Fortunio, the dandified widower with his morbid fidelity to the dead. The distinctive accents of moral censure are present in the plays from the outset, as Richard Alewyn has long since convincingly argued.[17] They are "moralities" in a modern, though no less proper sense of the term. It was not for nothing that Yeats subtitles *The Hour Glass* (1914) "a Morality," for in it he too dramatized one of the major problems of the age; the conflict between divine belief and unbelief. It has many points of similarity with Hofmannsthal's *Der Tor und der Tod*, not only in the simplicity of its formal structure, in its forceful emphasis on the ideas vested in the symbolic roles, but also in its recourse to the supernatural as the agent for revelation and moral insight. The figures of the Angel and of Death have comparable admonitory functions. Teigue and Claudio are both designated "Fools," though for contrary reasons. For Yeats the Fool is the vessel of higher wisdom, an oracular voice, whereas Claudio's name and title carry negative weight; he is intellectually clever (like Yeats's Wise Man, the teacher of rational truths) but spiritually and morally a cripple. The ominous sense of time running out is present in the very title of *The Hour Glass*, just as temporary urgency is introduced by the approach of Death in Hofmannsthal's play. Yeats gives the confrontation between the Wise Man and the Angel a strong dramatic tension, similar to the dialogue Claudio holds with Death, in that it is a contest for the soul. Both are being put to judgment by a higher authority. The dialectics of rational argument are in neither case a match for the

---

17 Richard Alewyn, *Über Hugo von Hofmannsthal*, Göttingen: Vandenhoeck & Ruprecht, 1958, p. 66, "Und darin ist dieses Werk unverstanden geblieben, daß, wie lyrisch immer seine Form, sein Sinn ein sittlicher ist" (it is just here that his oeuvre has remained misunderstood, that, however lyrical its form, it meaning is an ethical one).

powers of an absolute and non-contingent being. Yeats has the Angel say to the skeptic:

Angel: You have to die because no soul has passed
The heavenly threshold since you have opened school,
But grass grows there, and rust upon the hinge;
And they are lonely that must keep the watch.

Wise Man: And whither shall I go when I am dead?

Angel: You have denied there is a Purgatory,
Therefore the gate is closed; you have denied
There is a Heaven, and so that gate is closed.

Wise Man: Where then? For I have said there is no hell.

Angel: Hell is the place of those that have denied. (PI, 308 f.)

The Wise Man's efforts to find a single soul who can "say the creed with but a grain, a mustard seed of faith" (PI, 316) fails in a world he has taught to reason against faith. He cannot even bribe the Fool to divulge one syllable of his creed:

Wise Man: The last hope is gone,
And now that it's too late I see it all:
We perish into God and sink away
Into reality – the rest's a dream (PI, 322)

Such overt traditional religious symbolism is not employed in *Death and the Fool* (though Hofmannsthal later introduced it into his festival dramas). His figure of Death is not the harbinger of divine judgment but of a natural justice resulting from man's neglect of humanity. He is no figure of terror but enters into sensuous strains of the violin and speaks of his pervasive Dionysian presence in the ripeness of nature. His message, however, is addressed to the moral conscience:

> DER TOD
> Was allen ward auch dir gegeben,
> Ein Erdenleben, irdisch es zu leben.
> Im Innern quilt euch allen treu ein Geist,
> Der diesem Chaos toter Sachen
> Beziehung einzuhauchen heißt
> Und euren Garten draus zu machen
> Für Wirksamkeit Beglückung und Verdruß
> Weh dir, wenn ich dir das erst sagen muß!
> Man bindet und man wird gebunden. (GLD 281-2)

> (To you was given what all men receive,
> To live an earthly life by earthly means.
> Within you all a faithful spirit stirs
> Which prompts you to inspire this chaos
> Of dead things with vital meaning
> And to create of it your garden
> For active life, annoyance and delight.
> Woe to you, that I should have to tell you this!
> Man binds and he is also bound.)

Death teaches Claudio the lesson of what it means to be morally "bound" by letting the ghosts of his fruitless past parade before him. The Mother, the Girl and the Man, clear allegories of the closest human ties, address him accusingly in turn. Though his "conversion" comes too late to rescue him from Death, he achieves a final euphoric moment of moral illumination before his time is up. Awareness of the dimension of time is of the essence of this play, as is the case in most of Hofmannsthal's dramatic works. Consciousness of the passage of time, of its importance as a test of moral values, is a constant theme from *Gestern* onwards. The motif of "too late" reverberates like a solemn admonishment through his early works.

The symbolism of death is, of course, the ultimate recollection of time, and death is Hofmannsthal's major theme throughout, as Claudio Magris has observed.[18] In the wider context, this symbolism refers to the vanishing of an age, to that sense of an ending which expressed itself throughout Austrian culture at the turn of the century. In his unfinished play *Der Tod des Tizian* (1892 *The Death of Titian*) the ebbing away of life in the great artist assumes a deeper historical significance. The artist's death is portrayed as momentous, as marking the end of an era, and it leaves his pupils sorrowing in a world bereft of significance and beauty:

> Der Tizian sterben der das Leben schafft!
> Wer hätte dann zum Leben Recht und Kraft? (GLD, 254)

> (That Titian, life's creator, should die!
> Who then shall have the right and power to live?)

Such is the sustaining influence of the artist, that his death drains his pupils of vitality, hope and inspiration:

> Indessen wir zu schaffen nicht verstehen
> Und hilflos warten müssen der Enthüllung…
> Und unsre Gegenwart ist trüb und leer,
> Kommt uns die Weihe nicht von außen her. (GLD, 268)

> (While we no longer know how to create,
> And helplessly must wait for revelation…

---

18 Claudio Magris, *Der Habsburgische Mythos in der österreichischen Literatur*, Salzburg: Müller, 1988, p. 217.

And all or present days are bleak and void,
If no more benediction come to us.)

Hofmannsthal's representation of the power of the artist is achieved purely through the responses of his entourage; this reflexive device creates an aura which helps to raise him to mythical stature. There are a number of striking parallels to be drawn between this play and Yeats's tribute to the artist in *The Kings Threshold* (1904), which is also centrally concerned with the imminent death of the most honored of men, the poet Seanchan.[19] Yeats is equally concerned with the status of the artist in the realm, for the King who refuses the poet a seat in his council finally has to humble himself before "a mere man of words" (PI, 108). (One recalls that Yeats himself was made a Senator of the Irish Free State in 1922). By disdaining the King's food, the poet chooses death rather than the compromises and palliatives of political and worldly men. His sacred mission is marked by an uncompromising austerity. His pupils too are prepared to face death rather than bow to temporal pressures. The "king's threshold" which the poet and his pupils will not cross represents the resistant world of political power: this, notably, is the dimension absent from Hofmannsthal's play. As poet and playwright, Hofmannsthal consistently avoids direct engagement with the *realitas* of politics. Yeats's poet begins a suicidal hunger-strike

---

19 Hofmannsthal attempted a second, more conciliatory conclusion to his play (see "Nachtrag zum *Tod des Tizian*," GLD, 548-551) by introducing hopeful images of life's self-renewal; even so, the final word of the play, "vorbei," sounds a note of irrevocability.

such as has become very familiar to us in recent times. When Seabchan dies unvanquished, his jubilant youngest pupil shouts defiance at the king:

> Dead faces laugh!
> The ancient right is gone, the new remains,
> And that is death. (PI, 142)

These symbolic words, echoing the poet-leader's dying breath, have a chilling, prophetic ring to them in view of that indissoluble conjunction of poetry and politics in the subsequent history of Ireland. Whereas in Hofmannsthal's play death had signified dereliction and a loss of faith, Yeats ends on a note of political triumph and defiance.

The similarity between *The Shadowy Waters* and *Das Bergwerk zu Falun* (*The Mines at Falun*) has been remarked by Michael Hamburger as presenting "a parallel so uncannily close that one is tempted to attribute both plays to the workings of an international *Zeitgeist*."[20] Both Forgael and Elis are obsessed visionaries, estranged and solitary men, sailors who forsake their homes drawn by a restless impulse to find an alluring, unearthly love. In each case it is their daimon (Dectora and the Mountain Queen) who lures them to their doom with the promise of fulfillment. The threat of the dangerous unknown and ultimate death is as much invoked for dramatic purposes in Yeats's much compacter play as it is by Hofmannsthal's five acts, yet the accentuation of *The Shadowy Waters* is mystically romantic, whereas in

---

20 Michael Hamburger, op. cit., p. LVI.

Hofmannsthal it tends toward depth psychology; this very much reflects the intellectual climate of the Vienna of his day.[21] Hofmannsthal's imagery constantly refers to the maternal, to entering the earth, to mining: the deep mine into which Elis descends to find the Mountain Queen, suggests a journey of self-discovery, a delving into the unconscious mind. There are recognizably Freudian echoes in these subterranean caverns. The figure of Torbern the Miner, the boy Agmahd and the Fisherman's Son all function as mirror images of Elis: examples of that recurrence "der wechselseitigen Spiegelung" (reciprocal reflection) which Hofmannsthal saw in Goethean terms as a persistent pattern in his early work (A, 229). This tentative psychological symbolism tends to work as a disguise rather than as a veil to meaning. It tends to give Hofmannsthal's play a more fashionable, time-bound dimension than *The Shadowy Waters*, as his ruminatory diary entry in 1894 would appear to confirm: "Diese Spaltung des Ich scheint die Daseinsform des reproduzierenden Genies zu sein" (A, 115 This split in the ego seems to be the form of life proper to reproductive genius). Later, and with hindsight, he used the phrase "Analyse der dichterischen Existenz" (The analysis of the poetic existence" with reference to both *Das Bergwerk zu Falun* and *Der Kaiser und die Hexe* (A, 223). The role of volition and the unconscious, the divided self and the loss of

---

21 Hofmannsthal's interest on psychological reading at this and in later times may be seen reflected in his library. Cf. Michael Hamburger "Hofmannsthal's Bibliothek: Ein Bericht," *Euphorion*, 4th ser., vol. 55, 1961, pp. 26-31.

self, are psychological preoccupations worked into the symbolism of *Das Bergwerk zu Falun* more conspicuously than is usual with Hofmannsthal. He wrestled with the form for years, in much the same way as Yeats did with his play, to make it stageworthy (L, 460, 462). In either case it proved to be an important creative trial and it marks a transition to more dramatic writing.

Yeats wrote in 1905, after he had been revising his early plays:

> One thing I am now quite sure of is that all the finest poetry comes logically out of a fundamental action, and that the error of late periods like this is to believe that some things are inherently poetical, and to try to pull them on to the scene at every moment. It is just these seeming inherently poetical things that wear out (L, 460).

The symbolism introduced by Yeats and Hofmannsthal into their lyrical dramas was never so contrived nor so narrowly directed as to address only the passing historical moment. Their sense of the symbol as the natural emanation of poetry, and of the drama as mask and ritual, gave to their work a timeless dimension, a perpetuity of reference which belongs by definition to symbolism. As poets, they both stood firmly on the side of tradition and in an attitude of opposition to their times. As poets they also share an aura of solitude and self-assurance. Despite the acclaim each received from the best of their contemporaries, the figurative words Yeats noted in his Journal in 1909 speak for them both: "We artists, do not we also plant trees and it is only after some fifty years that we are of much value?" (Me, 156).

Variants of Social Comedy: Chekhov and *Der Schwierige* *

> *The laughter of the comedy is impersonal and of unrivalled politeness, nearer a smile; often no more than a smile. It laughs through the mind, for the mind directs it; and it might be called the humour of the mind.*
>
> —George Meredith, *An Essay on Comedy*

Any detailed comparison between writers of stature must inevitably involve investigation of contrasting features, for the truly important creative talent is by definition unique, and therefore essentially incomparable. In the case of Chekhov and Hofmannsthal, the very accidents of historical proximity (Hofmannsthal was fourteen years Chekhov's junior), their keen and persistent interest in the possibilities of the theater, no less than certain finer points of similarity in their sense of dramatic form and in artistic sensibility, might urge to look more closely at what appears disparate, in order to discover common ground in their respective approaches to comedy, as well as to draw distinctions. And the act of drawing distinctions is itself designed to illuminate and establish certain correspondences. The bias of

---

* Textual references to Chekhov's works are to the edition: *Polnoe Sobranie Sočinenü i Pisem v Tridcati Tomax*, Moscow, 1974 ff., abbreviated PSS.

attention must, in the present context, fall on Hofmannsthal's achievement in the comedy of his mature period, and specifically in *Der Schwierige* (*The Difficult Man*) which he himself called a "Gesellschaftslustspiel" (social comedy) and where he clearly stands closest to Chekhov.[1] Hofmannsthal retrospectively reflected on his creative development as a gradual progress towards an increasing involvement in the social world. That he saw the comedy as the form which most completely fulfilled these artistic aspirations is attested by the much-quoted assertion in *ad me ipsum* "Das erreichte Soziale: die Komödien" (A, 226 the social

---

1 letter from Hofmannsthal to Leopold von Andrian, October 4, 1917, refers to "meine Gesellschaftskomödie, die unter wohl erzogenen Menschen spielt" (my social comedy which is set among well-bred people), cf also his letter to Arthur Schnitzler, November 2, 1919 in *Briefwechsel*, Frankfurt am Main: Fischer, 1964, p. 287. Hofmannsthal's early notes on *Der Schwierige* indicate his wavering between the designation "Charactercomödie" with no more than "eine Kette von Gesprächen" (a series of conversations) and a "Gesellschaftscomödie," "mit der Figur des "Schwierigen" als Mittelpunkt" (with the figure of *The Difficult Man* at the heart); "Keime des Lustspiels. Frühe Notizen zum 'Schwierigen' und zum 'Unbestechlichen'," mitgeteilt von Leonhard M. Fiedler in HB, 25, 1982, pp. 77 f. A comparison with Chekhov has been attempted by Theo Reucher, "Selbstmörder und Clown: Zum Verfall allgemeiner Kommunikations- und Handlungsmöglichkeiten in Tschechows *Iwanow* und Hofmannsthals *Der Schwierige*," *Literatur für Leser*, vol. 1, 1979, pp. 45-66. The approach is strictly thematic, analyzing "die tödliche Krankheit einer Gesellschaft" (the fatal malady of a society) in relation to both plays, and paying almost no regard to either irony in the language or to formal elements of the comedy. A more sensitive comparison, though transcending the limits of comedy, may be found in Dominique Iehl, "Le prince Muichkine, Karl Bühl, Ulrich ou de quelques qualités de héros sans qualités," EG, 29e année, no. 2, avril-juin 1974, pp. 179-191.

idea attained: the comedies). What precisely he meant by "das Soziale" or "das Gesellschaftliche" (the social idea), and how this differs from Chekhov's understanding, remains to be explored.[2]

The immense contribution made by Chekhov to the modern drama and to our sense of comic theater is today beyond question. He has established in our consciousness aesthetic criteria by which we are accustomed to judge drama and which have acquired for us the natural status of ideal norms. Yet even this great innovator of the modern stage does not autonomously introduce new forms of the comedy, but owes a substantial debt to his Russian precursors; to Gogol, that most satirical depicter of corrupt society, to Griboyedov, that subtle analyst of the psyche and creator of Chatsky, to Turgenev, the master of "polyphonic" dialogue and lyricism of mood, to Ostrovsky, the realist who typifies Russian character in his full blooded theatrical portraits. It is above all the complex, diversified and historically defined image of society, a society explored with critical, often satirical penetration, which the Russian comedy has left to posterity. Chekhov was notoriously

---

2   Richard Alewyn, *Über Hugo von Hofmannsthal*, Göttingen: Vandenhoeck & Ruprecht, 1958, p. 80 displays his usual discrimination in qualifying Hofmannsthal's sense of "das Soziale" with the phrase "in der Naturform des Geselligen oder in der Kunstform des Gesellschaftlichen" (in its natural form as the convivial, or in art as the social idea). Critics have generally trended to dwell on conceptual, formal and thematic aspects of *Der Schwierige* (e. g. Staiger, Mennemeier, Emrich, Steffen, Rosch, Kobel), rather than the social. William E. Yates provides a most helpful definitive statement on "the social milieu" in his critical edition *Der Schwierige*, Cambridge: Cambridge University Press, 1966, pp. 24-27.

modest and self-disparaging whenever he spoke of his dramatic gift. He saw himself chiefly as a writer of prose and would point to an Ibsen or a Hauptmann as his notion of genuine dramatic talent on the contemporary stage. The fact that he, and later Hofmannsthal, were destined to represent another, quite distinct form of drama in which inner conflicts were explored not by outward action, but by a diversity of other, subtler means of theatrical expression, was not fully registered by him. It was, furthermore, Chekhov who was foremost in establishing on the stage that complex form of drama interfusing the tragic with the comic which had become a hallmark of modern theater, which has formed our sensibilities and guided our tastes. The contentious problem of comedy as a genre has been most searchingly confronted by the author of *The Seagull* and *The Cherry Orchard* (both of which are entitled comedies), while he wavered over *Ivanov*, calling it first a comedy and then settling for the neutral designation "drama" which he also applied to *Three Sisters*. *Platonov* (published posthumously in 1923 under the title *Besotcovščina*) might well, like *Uncle Vania*, be sub-titled "Scenes of Country Life," for it shows up especially well the problematical nature of Chekhovian comedy as an ostensibly plotless play peopled with fatuous failures who engage in desultory conversation and remain hopelessly enmeshed in the painful futility of social existence. *Uncle Vania* too, in its original version *The Wood Demon*, was designated a comedy by its author. For such reasons, Chekhov's use of the term comedy has been judged "loose and idiosyncratic."[3] The complex

---

3 Ronald Hingley, *The Oxford Chekhov*, Oxford: Oxford University

ambivalence involved in the application of the genre reflects the temper of the age and seems peculiarly characteristic for the indeterminate kind of social comedy which Chekhov created, and to which Hofmannsthal later contributed his own, highly individual, variants. Without wishing to adopt Helmut Arntzen's term "die ernste Komödie" (serious comedy), or yet to ignore the merits of Karl Guthke's fundamental definition of modern "tragi-comedy," I am inclined to abide by the designation "comedy" where the authors themselves have adopted it even where the Muse

---

Press, 1967, vol. 2, p. 8, Richard D. Risso, "Chekhov: A View of the Basic Ironic Structures," *Chekhov's Great Plays: A Critical Anthology*, New York and London: New York University Press, 1981, pp. 181-188 is sensitive to the interplay of the pathetic and the "ironically comic" situations in the playwright. Franz Norbert Mennemeier, *Das moderne Drama des Auslandes*, Düsseldorf: Bagel, 1961, p. 12, puts the beginnings and the dissolution of the comic genre "seit Pirandello, im Grunde aber schon seit Büchners *Leonce und Lena* (since Pirandello, but actually already since Büchner's *Leonce and Lena*). He also identifies the close interdependence of formal and social factors, so significant for the modern comedy (p. 129): "Die Komödienform (oder was ihr entspricht) hat nicht zufällig fast überall im modernen Theater die Krise der gesellschaftlich-geselligen Wirklichkeit, auf die sie mehr als jede andere Literaturgattung angewiesen ist, als Thema und dramaturgisches Prinzip in sich hineingenommen. Das gilt selbst von einem Drama wie Hugo von Hofmannsthals Lustspiel *Der Schwierige*, diesem letzten großen Beispiel einer formal bewältigten, äußerlich realistischen Komödie." (It is no accident that comedy as a form [or whatever corresponds to it] has almost everywhere in modern theater taken up as its theme and dramaturgical principle the crisis within social-convivial reality, on which it depends more than any other literary genre. *The Difficult Man*, that last great example of a formally resolved, outwardly realistic comedy.)

Thalia has proved fickle or inconstant.[4] If we find Dr. Samuel Johnson's classic definition of comedy as "a laughable dramatic piece" tantalizingly cryptic, he further assures us that "laughable" means "exciting laughter, droll," and, if we press him further, he instructs us that "laughter" signifies "a convulsive merry noise."[5] Whether Chekhov or Hofmannsthal are primarily to be defined by the inducement of such a noise or not, their contribution to the modern form of comic theater seems assured.

Comedy can, but need not, depend on drama for its momentum and vitality. The dramatic construct, the well-conceived plot, is not the indispensible motor of good comic theater. It may indeed be claimed that the comic character, fully conceived and portrayed in theatrical terms (such as we find in Molière), is more important than the invention of a plot and that the plots of comedy are traditionally trivial and artificial constructs where accident and

---

4 Helmut Arntzen, *Die ernste Komödie: Das deutsche Lustspiel von Lessing bis Kleist*, Munich, 1968, pp. 18 f., writes with some reservation about the concept "tragi-comedy": Bedeutet Tragikomödie anderes, als daß in die Komödie Momente aufgenommen werden können, die innerhlb der Tragödie tragisch funktionieren, bedeutet der Begriff nichts. Denn sie zur Synthese führen heißt Tragödie und Komödie auflösen." (If tragicomedy means anything more than that elements may be assimilated into comedy which in tragedy have a tragic function, then the concept has no meaning. For to bring them to a synthesis is to dissolve tragedy and comedy.) Karl S. Guthke, *Die moderne Tragikomödie: Theorie und Gestalt*, Göttingen: Vandenhoeck & Ruprecht, 1968, p. 120, points with more assurance to Chekhov as the dramatist, "Dem wir eine der gelungensten Tragikomödien der Weltliteratur verdanken" (to whom we owe the most successful tragi-comedies of world literature.)
5 Samuel Johnson, A Dictionary of the English Language, Enlarged Edition, Edinburgh, 1822.

coincidence play a significant part.[6] Chekhov and Hofmannsthal both had considerable problems in executing the dramatic plot. Chekhov wrote in despair in 1892: "The endings won't come! The hero either marries or shoots himself. There is no other way out."[7] He seems to have preferred the second way out; most of his plays end with a pistol shot. By the same token, Hofmannsthal's correspondence with Strauss reveals the constant struggle to produce a more forceful dramatic line and more "drastic" effects in his writing for the stage.[8] The plotless, but not actionless play, understood as a concatenation of episodic scenes, each exploring and adding further dimensions to the interplay of human relations, is the blueprint for the Chekhovian comedy and it equally defines the form of *Der Schwierige*. A basic affinity between the creators of

---

6 Wylie Sypher, "The Meanings of Comedy," George Meredith, *Comedy*, Garden City NJ: Doubleday, 1956, p. 219, "Comedy remains an 'improvisation' with a loose structure and a precarious logic that can tolerate every kind of 'improbability'." The point about random plots is perhaps most consummately made by a publication by Georg Nikolaus Bärmann (d 1850) which is nothing more than a compilation of fragmentary exchanges, the random sequence of which may be determined merely by throwing a dice, entitled: *Neunhundert neun und neunzig und etliche Almanachs-Lustspiele durch den Würfel*, Zwickau: Schumann, 1829 (*Nine Hundred and Ninety and Sundry Almanach-Comedies at a Dice-Throw*.)
7 Letter to A. S. Souvorin, June 4, 1892, *Letters on the Short Story, The Drama and other Literary Topics by Anton Chekhov*, selected and edited by Louis S. Friedland, New York: Dover, 1964, pp. 117 f.
8 Richard Strauss, Hugo von Hofmannsthal, *Briefwechsel*, herausgegeben von Franz und Alice Strauss, Zurich: Atlantis, 1952: à propos *Der Rosenkavalier*, pp. 60 ff., and particularly p. 71 where the distinction is debated between "dem bloß Heiteren und dem drastisch Komischen" (the merely cheerful in the drastically comic).

Platonov, Ivanov and Hans Karl is indicated by the fact that these characters are conceived in essentially passive terms; an innate passivity of temperament, be it nonchalance, apathy, chronic indecision, or sheer ineptitude in social relations, is the common denominator between them. Indeed, one is tempted to claim that Hans Karl has much of the Slav in him and would not look out of place in that succession of figures representing "the superfluous man" (lišnij čelovek) in Russian literature. It is characteristic of both writers to think primarily in terms of a whole gallery of miniature portraits to be worked into *The Wood Demon* and he finds it necessary to explicate the chief figures of *Ivanov* in a lengthy letter.[9] His *Note-Books* constitute a reservoir of embryonic material which helps to shed light on his dramatic method. For there he records the nucleus of a conception for his work; very often it is merely a comic name which is evocative of certain traits, or an incongruous remark which suggests a peculiar speaker or situation, for instance: "Mammy, don't show yourself to the guests, you are very fat," or "it's an abscess that's just burst inside you…, it's all right, have some more vodka," or "what does your husband do?" "He takes castor oil."[10] Hofmannsthal offers an interesting parallel instance in a letter to Schnitzler where he probes the sources of creative stimulus whilst describing his own method of working:

---

9   Letter to A. S. Souvorin, December 30, 1888, Letters by Anton Checkhov, as above, pp. 134-141.
10 *The Notebooks of Anton Tchekhov together with Reminiscences of Tchekhov by Maxim Gorki*, translated by S. S. Koteliansky and Leonard Woolf, London: Hogarth, 1967, pp. 64, 67, 70.

Was ich aus späteren Acten vorausarbeiten kann, sind nicht geschlossene Scenen, sondern reine Farbenskizzen: Worte und Dialogstellen, die oft gar nicht wirkich aufgenommen werden, mir aber als Parfumflaschen, als Stimmungs-Accumulatoren und −Condensatoren dienen, damit die Suggestion im Laufe der Detailarbeit nicht verloren geht.[11]

(What I can work up in advance for later Acts are not finished scenes but pure colored sketches; words and scraps of dialogue which are often not taken up at all, but which serve me as little bottles of scent, as mood accumulators and condensers, so that the power of suggestion does not get lost in the course of work on detail.)

Again it is the smallest particles of language, fragments of dialogue, words, incoherent in themselves but highly evocative to the dramatist, which become significant from the time of inception and are worked into a form which is digressive, intermittent and composed of a plurality of points of emphasis. This new form of comedy with its looser composition is not to be compared with the taut bow-string of drama, but is a subtler, less conspicuous construct in which a diversity of tensions and contrasts replace the unified continuum of their own. *Der Schwierige* may just as much be characterized by "that inner line" or again, the "line of inner action" which Stanislavsky saw as the salient feature of the Chekhov play.[12] The finding of this inner line or uniting principle, which provides such a challenge to actors and interpreters

---

11 Hofmannsthal Schnitzler, p. 26.
12 Constantin Stanislavsky, *My Life in Art*, 4th ed., London: Geoffrey Bles, 1945, p. 353.

alike, has much to do with establishing the tone and the precise mood, as Stanislavsky was to discover in training his actors. The dramatic import of so much of what passes between characters is expressed at the more subdued level of nuance, intimation, half-statement and eloquent silences. The whole concern with live performance becomes unusually acute in this form of theater and that is the reason why Hofmannsthal was so anxious to see his comedies performed by particular actors and why he withheld *Der Schwierige* from the German stage for three years, hoping that Max Reinhardt might be its first producer.[13]

One might see something almost providential in the close and continuing involvement of two of the most innovative figures of the contemporary theater, Stanislavsky and Reinhardt, with the work of Chekhov and Hofmannsthal respectively, for this historical coincidence greatly helped to bring the work of both playwrights to the forefront of public attention. It gave the new social comedy which they, in their separate ways, were evolving, the cachet of modernity through the authority and distinction of performance. When Hofmannsthal mentions his own comedy alongside Chekhov's plays as Reinhardt's choice of "moderns" (A, 277 f), it indicates that he evidently thought of *Der Schwierige* in the context of forward-looking theater which was exploring new formal possibilities. In March 1924 he reports on Reinhardt's forthcoming season of plays at the Theater in der Josefsstadt which was to include: "ein Lustspiel von mir, durch welches er die Linie des modernen Gesellschaftsstückes repräsentiert" (A, 322

---

13 Hofmannsthal to Wildgans, H/Wildgans, p. 31.

a comedy of mine by which he is representing the line taken by the modern social play). Clearly then, Hofmannsthal wished to draw attention to the innovative conception of *Der Schwierige* and to see it ranged alongside such moderns as Strindberg, O'Neill and, of course, Chekhov ("einige Russen, unter denen natürlich Tschechov," A, 322 a number of Russians, among these naturally Chekhov). The addition of the word "naturally" indicates how established the Russian playwright's reputation on the world stage had become by 1924.

The traditionalist leanings of Hofmannsthal's dramaturgy generally receive more critical attention than the newness or modernity of his treatment. Juxtaposition with Chekhov's technique of comedy helps us to see more clearly Hofmannsthal's decidedly original approach to the play without a well-defined plot, in which little changes and virtually nothing happens. Social existence consists of a number of random encounters, conversations or exchanges, of misunderstandings and aggravations perhaps, but the general tenor of life is shown to be banal and pedestrian. The avoidance of the grandiose or sensational is programmatic. The focus is on the <u>minutiae</u> of psychological interplay, on the constantly fluctuating tone of social intercourse, on the subtleties of verbal and mimic communication. By concentrating attention on an assorted, individuated group of characters, all theatrically drawn with varying degrees of detail or sympathy, talking, flirting and having their being within a sharply defined social and historical environment, the electric field of irony is of itself established. One may be reminded of Schopenhauer's *Psychologische*

Bemerkungen where he crisply observed about society: "jeder trägt eine Maske und spielt eine Rolle. Überhaupt ist das ganze gesellschaftliche Leben ein fortwährendes Komödienspielen"[14] (Everyone wears a mask and performs a role, in fact, the whole of social life is one continuing game of comedy). Hofmannsthal shared this sense of the social fabric as the ready-made ground for ironic comedy. In *Die Lästigen* (1916) polite society is compared to a precious carpet: "dieses Gewebe aus lächerlicher Anmaßung, aus Standesdünkel, aus Geldstolz" (LII, 122 This web of ludicrous presumption, arrogance of rank and pride in money). As he remarked in "Die Ironie der Dinge" (1921: "die wirkiche Komödie setzt ihre Individuen in ein tausendfach verhäkeltes Verhältnis zur Welt, sie setzt alles in ein Verhältnis zu allem, und damit alles in ein Verhältnis der Ironie" (PIV, 40 True comedy places its individual figures in a thousand interlaced relationships with the world, it places everything in relation to the world, it places everything in relation to everything else and thus everything within a context of irony). This all-pervading irony or, in his words, "Element so allseitiger Ironie" (PIV, 43 element of such all-round irony) constitutes the more rarified intellectual climate which vitalizes the specific style of his social comedy. His signature is the semblance of realism, the subtle contrivance of a seeming authenticity in the social image he projects. His art has more of the artificial distancing of irony in it than Chekhov's, whose theater invokes feeling to

---

14 Artur Schopenhauer, *Artur Schopenhauers sämtliche Werke*, Großherzog Wilhelm Ernst Ausgabe, herausgegeben von Eduard Grisebach, Leipzig: Reclam, 1920, p. 640.

a greater extent and therefore more closely engages our sympathies, Chekhov's greater realism also allows the tragic to surface naturally through its comic style, and as he is more generously attuned to the emotions he can work upon feelings of compassion without ever becoming partisan.[15] Chekhov's proverbial truthfulness to life does not shut out intensity of feeling any more than it can omit the manifold ironies implicit in the vagaries of social conversation. For both playwrights irony is a highly significant part of the comic form, though it takes on a different quality in their respective hands.

The importance Hofmannsthal attached to the ironic mode as the sustaining element in comedy is given increased significance by his choice of historical context. Here he follows the Chekhovian pattern by placing *Der Schwierige* in a strictly contemporary setting. It is the only comedy in which he does so. *Der Unbestechliche* (1923 *The Incorruptible Man*) is still set in the pre-war era when gentility was commonly measured by the degree of effete dependence upon the serving classes. What results from this choice of the concluding phase of World War I (the

---

15 Harvey Pitcher, "The Chekhov Play," Chekhov New Perspectives, edited by René and Nonna D. Wellek, Englewood Cliffs N J: Prentice-Hall, 1984, states: "What happens in the course of the Chekhov play is that the characters are shown responding and reacting to one another on the emotional level: Chekhov creates what may be called an emotional network, in which it is not the interplay of character but the interplay of emotion that holds the attention of the audience" (p. 79). Though this view allows for no irony in Chekhov's treatment, it generally holds good and may be contrasted with Hofmannsthal's more detached ironic treatment of social relations.

date for the setting has been suggested as September 12, 1917) is an implicit intrusion of ironic comment which contrasts the historical cataclysms of revolutionary change with the unshakable self-assurance of an obsolete social order that continues to behave as if nothing in their world had changed.[16] This unbelievable detachment or supreme indifference (it is never quite certain which it is) in the former ruling classes has, in itself, some comic potential which is not actually exploited. The world of graver hostilities beyond the salon is kept at bay and only mentioned in passing or distantly referred to as "da draußen" (out there). It is a similar subversive irony which we find in *The Cherry Orchard*, where the Ranevsky household, bankrupt and superseded by the mercenary Lopakhins of a new age, persists in its vanities and futile pursuit of pleasure even as the axe is laid to the root of the trees. Only in Chekhov the mundane and material realities crowd into the dialogue and we are never allowed to forget that the old order is in dissolution. An implacable realism informs his image of society and his use of irony has been called "tough and brutal."[17]

Hofmannsthal's treatment of society is more tentative and suggestive. At Altenwyl's soirée, a social gathering comparable to many a scene in Chekhov, Neuhoff is moved to remark:

---

16 Wolfgang Frühwald, "Die sprechende Zahl: Datensymbolismus in Hugo von Hofmannsthals Lustspiel *Der Schwierige*," JDSG, 22, 1978, pp. 572-588, see also Martin Stern, "Wann entstand und spielt *Der Schwierige*?" JDSG, 23, 1979, pp. 350-365, where he relies to Frühwald's article, both in terms of a corrective and in amplification.
17 Donald Rayfield, *Chekhov: The Evolution of His Art*, London: Elek, 1975, p. 7.

> Alle diese Menschen, die Ihnen hier begegnen, existieren ja in Wirklichkeit gar nicht mehr. Das sind ja alles nur mehr Schatten. Niemand, der sich in diesen Salons bewegt, gehört zu der wirklichen Welt, in der die geistigen Krisen des Jarhunderts sich entscheiden. (LII, 230)
>
> (All these people you meet with here do not in reality exist any more. They are actually no more than shadows. No one who goes about these salons belongs to the real world in which the intellectual crises of the century are being resolved.)

Neuhoff is but one voice in the play, that of the outsider to this unreal society, the conceited Prussian who feels he can pass judgment on all he sees. Yet what he says has, like so much of Hofmannsthal's dialogue, significance at two levels. Neuhoff is asserting that this society has outlived its day, that it has ceased to have any significance politically or ideologically. It exists only in self-delusion as a kind of shadowy charade. At the same time his words contain a disguised allusion to the fictive nature of social reality within the play. The characters are the invented shadows of the creative imagination; their representative status and cunningly disguised artificiality are the products of fine artistic calculation. Hofmannsthal was not a Naturalist. His dramatic technique was suggestive rather than representational, allusive rather than mimetic; and he was given to symbolic statement as he tells us in his aphorism: "Wer das Gesellschaftliche anders als symbolisch nimmt, geht fehl" (A, 21 Whoever perceives the social ideal in other than symbolic terms, misses the truth). Or again, he once noted: "Das Gesellschaftliche kann und darf man nur allegorisch nehmen. Hier läßt sich das ganze Gesellschaftliche der neueren Zeit (von Lessing und der Sévigné an) als eine große Mythologie zusammenfassen" (A, 27 The social idea can and must only be understood allegorically. This is where the whole social idea of more recent times [from Lessing and Mme. de Sévigné onwards] may be subsumed in one great mythology). These notions are amplified by his friend the essayist Carl J. Burckhardt in his memoirs of 1914:

> Als er das Lustspiel *Der Schwierige* schrieb, hat er sich eine Lebensatmosphäre vorgezogen oder gar in der Hauptfigur etwa – wie gesagt worden ist – sich selbst gesetzt und bespiegelt. Nein, in diesem Stück wollte er einer sozialen schicht, dem imperial spanisch-deutschen Hochadel Österreichs, auf dem Wege des Sichtbarmachens durch eine leichte Übertreibung, ein Denkmal im Augenblick seines Auflösens und Versinkens setzen.

(When he wrote the comedy *The Difficult Man*, he did not give preference to the atmosphere of his own life, nor indeed – as has been said – produce and mirror himself in the principal figure. No, in this play he wanted to raise a monument to a social class, the imperial Spanish-German aristocracy of Austria just at the point of its dissolution and passing, by making it visible through slight exaggeration.)[18]

The act of delicately capturing the salient features of a vanishing society at a specific point in history is nicely expressed by Burckhardt. Hofmannsthal's wish to hold to the last vestiges of

---

18 Carl J. Burckhardt, *Erinnerungen an Hofmannsthal und Briefe des Dichters*, Basel: Schwabe, 1944, p. 33.

a society which was highly cultivated, tradition-bound, rather quaint and colorful in deportment and language, actually lies at the root of his creative endeavor. In one significant sense, then, he too wished to "write his times" by writing this comedy much in the way of Chekhov, but with more than a hint of nostalgia. By choosing the critical moment in history when a particular culture had outlived itself, he enlisted anachronism; and anachronism serves both as a spur to irony and, inevitably, as a potent ingredient of comedy.

Der Schwierige offers a rarified image of a select section of Viennese society, a privileged group that were played out and yet continued to perform their parts, acting out roles into which birth and breeding had cast them. The verb "spielen" (to play) permeates the dialogue and suggests the anachronistic make-believe of social intercourse. Emulation of outmoded social conduct, with its posing and theatricality in those circles, in fact goes some way to meeting the demands of the comic playwright. The sense of authenticity of atmosphere, naturalness of conversation, absence of distortion in characterization (apart from minor caricatures) stamp this play as sustained high comedy with scarcely a trace of farce in it. Above all the high sophistication of language, with its abundance of French loan words, clearly signals a high degree of artistry. More than anything else in the play, language is the carrier of that social image and atmosphere. Carl J. Burckhardt has written: "Im Übrigen ist in diesem Stück – wie in jeder Hervorbringung des Dichters – die soziale Atmosphäre nur die Tonart, in welcher ein großer geistig-menschliche Vorgang komponiert ist."[19] (In this play, incidentally – as in every one of the poet's products – the social atmosphere is merely the key in which a great spiritual-human process has been composed). The critical verdict on what is focal and what is peripheral to the comedy, accords very much with what Hofmannsthal himself committed in his diary in 1926: "Im 'Schwierigen' Andeutung des Verhältnisses zwischen Phantasiegestalten und der Realität. Das Soziale – perspektivisch behandelt." (A, 237 In *The Difficult Man*, a hint of the relationship between figures of the imagination and reality. The social idea – treated by means of perspectives). The conviction that "reality" (whatever one might mean by that) is not to be embodied within the play, that it cannot be translated wholesale onto the stage in the manner advocated by thoroughgoing Naturalists, but remains an illusory category to be treated with the playwright's capacity for illusion, gives rise to a different approach; namely that of a selective perspectivism. The illusion of a complete unit of society, differentiated and full of interesting contrasts, of differing circumstances, levels of intelligence and points of view, is produced by Hofmannsthal through a kaleidoscopic technique of ever-shaping groupings and relationships. Here the proximity to Checkhov's method is given. The forty-eight scenes which make up the three acts of *Der Schwierige*, display an ever shifting pattern of "Bezüge" (correlations – to use a favorite term of Hofmannthal's), of significant links between the sixteen characters. These groupings and relationships are finely gauged for their ironic effect. Social attitudes are contrasted, views are

---

19 Carl J. Burckhardt, *Erinnerungen an Hugo von Hofmannsthal*, p. 34,

exchanged on anything from politics to mysticism, from war to wedlock and from art to acrobatics. The much-mentioned art of conversation which polite society indulges in, becomes the mirror in which it relishes its own reflection. Conversation is practiced with more than a touch of self-conscious vanity. The airs and graces assumed in Altenwyl's soirée by most of the secondary characters give a very illuminating view of the aspirations, prejudices and vanities of each speaker. Clearly Hofmannsthal has updated and adapted established features of the Viennese "Konversationsstück" (comedy of manners). Conventions are opposed to the unconventional, posing to sincerity, pretentiousness to veracity, philandering to love. A seemingly endless progression of refracted perspectives is opened up as this society is explored through different encounters, formal and informal, arranged and accidental.

Above all, the old and the new order at this historical watershed are brought into confrontation, just as Chekhov does by the introduction of characters like Bugrov, Borkin and Lopakhin who jarr on their environment with their vulgarity and brashness. Even the names Hofmannsthal gives certain characters point to such an intention. The effete old aristocracy is typified in Altenwyl, while the new order is suggested in Neuhoff, Neugebauer and Vinzenz (originally called Nowak). The opening scene of the play is a perfect exposition of this latent social conflict, as the retiring manservant Lukas, the very image of his master in discretion, decency and decorum, attempts the hopeless task of instructing Vinzenz, the uncouth, inquisitive aspirant, in the mysteries of serving so "difficult" a master. Vinzenz stands for an age which tramples politeness and finesse underfoot; he is blunt in his directness and brash in his ambition. At a higher level of sophistication, Neuhoff represents a variant of that intrusive alien mentality; he typifies the disturbing onslaught of the cult of manliness and domination based on the will. Hans Karl says of him: "Er hat Geist aber es wird einem nicht wohl dabei" (LII, 197 He has intellect, but it hardly makes one comfortable). Altenwyl's introduction of Neuhoff as "der einzige Vertreter des Geistes in einem rein sozialen Milieu" (LII, 215-216 The sole representative of intellect in a purely social milieu) conveys a more ironic point of distinction than he knows. Elsewhere Stani protests: "Aber ich bitte: so viele Taktlosigkeiten als Worte (LII, 196 Well I ask you: no fewer *fauxpas* than words). And Antoinette rebuffs him with: "Ihr kalter, wollender Verstand hebt ja den Kopf aus dem Wort, das Sie reden: (LII, 281 Your cold, designing reason raises its head in every word you utter). Predictably, Helene too rejects the hollow rhetoric and pathos of his advances. One detects in this rejection something of that polemic entitled "Preuße und Österreicher" (1917 "The Prussian and the Austrian") in which Hofmannsthal, with ill-disguised political bias, attempted to draw sharp distinctions between the two cultures. Such typologizing works well within comedy but appears as a somewhat inept polemic in purely abstract form. Since Hofmannsthal's rather fervid writings on Austria fall within the period of the First World War, and the inception of *Der Schwierige* coincides with these preoccupations, the social significance of the figure of Neuhoff, typifying certain aspects of an alien Nordic outlook, is intriguingly topical. The third character who presents a contrast to traditional social attitudes and values is Neugebauer (a common name in Vienna which still fills a good page of the city's telephone directory today). He is the opportunist with an ample streak of ruthlessness in him, disguised by deferential manners and speech. His language is an odd mélange of suave ready-to-hand phrasing, part "Kanzleideutsch" (officialese), part "Salonsprache" (the language of the salon), which aspires to the polish of the cultured classes but succeeds only in attaining "Bildungsjargon" (the jargon of the semi-educated):

> NEUGEBAUER: Ich habe schon seit einiger Zeit die Bemerkung gemacht, daß etwas an mir neuerdings Euer Erlaucht zur Ungeduld reizt. Allerdings war mein Bildungsgang ganz auf das Innere gerichtet, und wenn ich vielleicht keine tadellosen Salonmanieren erworben habe, so wird dieser Mangel vielleicht in den Augen eines wohlwollenden Beurteilers aufgewogen werden können durch Qualitäten, die persönlich hervorheben zu müßen meinem Charakter allerdings nicht leicht fallen würde. (LII, 172-173)

> (I have for some time past remarked that there is something about me which has of late aroused your Lordship's impatience. True, my path to an education has led inward, and if perhaps I have not acquired immaculate salon manners in the process, then this deficiency may perhaps be made good in the eyes of a benevolent judge by qualities which I would hardly find it in my character to need to underline myself).

The stiff pretentiousness, the pedantic syntax, the superfluous emotive particle "allerdings" and "vielleicht" all point to an inner haughtiness and presumption. Social aspirations in a world where the old order has become invalid are implicit in the grudging respect, the over-ready punctiliousness, the personal hyper-sensitivity exuded by this confidential secretary. An adept modern offshoot of Uriah Heep, he betrays his callous egotism most bluntly when he is questioned about his fiancée. It seems that he jilted her for another girl, "Tochter eines höheren Beamten" (daughter of a high-ranking official) who had suddenly become eligible upon the death of her betrothed at the front. Honoring this "heiliges Vermächtnis" (sacred legacy) of a fallen friend by stepping into his shoes is presented by Neugebauer as one of the more acceptable spoils of war. On receiving this intelligence, Hans Karl asks: "Und die frühere langjährige Beziehung? Neugebauer: Ich habe sie natürlich gelöst. Selbstverständlich in der vornehmsten und gewissenhaftesten Weise." (LII, 174 And what of the previous long-standing relationship? Neugebauer: Naturally I cut that off. Obviously in the most dignified and conscientious way possible). His tone is disarmingly pragmatic; "natürlich" and "selbstverständlich" do service for explanations. Whatever material arrangements have been made to console the abandoned fiancée of five years; standing and waiting, they are alluded to in a manner which attempts to combine noblesse with practicality in two suave superlatives: "vornehmsten" and "gewissenhaftesten." It is tempting to see in these twin qualifications the contradiction between the old order and the new which Neugebauer is attempting to reconcile by giving respectability to rank opportunism. It is the unprincipled social climber by the matrimonial ladder who stands before us, unmasked by irony. In focusing on the social perspectives that open out by scrutiny of the secondary figures of the comedy, one is inadvertently shifting the emphasis away from the central figure, a man who is both the soul of discretion and the cause of rampant confusion, both guilelessly obliging and incorrigibly "difficile." But of course the whole network of social relationships. Intrigue, match-making, disparaging gossip and speculation, are all centered on Hans Karl the full-blown social enigma, "der Mann ohne Absichten" (the man without intentions) as Hofmannsthal originally called him. He remains at the center of speculation and comment, while these represent reflections or distortions of his complex personality. Hofmannsthal was, characteristically, attempting to achieve two goals in writing the comedy; to portray a profound and elusive personality at the hub of the dramatic construct and at the same time to provide a differentiated image of the society to which he intimately belongs.[20] He felt that he had just about succeeded in subordinating any subjective features, "das Bekenntnishafte" (the confessional element) at the core of the work, to the social

---

20 Letter to Rudolph Pannwitz, August 22, 1917, "Aus Hofmannthals Brief an Rudolph Pannwitz," herausgegeben von Herbert Steiner, *Mesa*, no. 5, Lexington KY: Jacob Hammer, 1955, p. 26: "für die nächste Phase ist es die Comödie, in der ich mich geben und finden muß, in ihr kann ich meine Elemente zusammenfassen: das Einsame und das Soziale. Das Mystische und das Dialektische, Sprache nach innen und Sprache nach außen" (for the next stage it is comedy to which I must devote and in which I must find myself, in it I can gather all the elements of my being: solitude and the social aspect, the mystical and the dialectical, language directed inwards and outwards).

dimension by means of irony as the overriding formal element. A letter to Anton Wildgans (February 14, 1921) confesses: "und doch ist dieser individuell-metaphysische Kern sehr stark, und mir ist manchmal Angst gewesen, er durchbräche mir die Hülle," (and yet this individual-metaphysical core is very strong, and I was at times afraid that it would break its mould).[21] In terms of its critical reception by posterity, the author need not have worried. The confessional note is not obtrusive nor does the play possess even the low-key metaphysical accents of his last comedy *Der Unbestechliche*.

The ironic mode establishes that uncommitted, that vaguely detached stance, "dieses gewisse Etwas von Superiorität" (LII, 310 This subtle hint of superiority) within the figure of Hans Karl, which not merely colors the tone and texture of the comedy but also affects the very fabric of social relationships. Haltung: sozial-östrreichische ("der feine kluge Wiener" Attitude: social Austrian [the "refined intelligent Viennese"]) reads Hofmannsthal's diary of November 5, 1926, as he identifies the ironic stance he had adopted to convey Hans Karl's demeanor: "Haltung des 'Schwierigen' in einer nuancelosen Welt" (A, 239 Attitude of *The Difficult Man* in a world without nuance). By contrast with Hans Karl's subtle complexity, the social world represented by the guests at Altenwyl's soirée is lacking in nuance, marked out and motivated as it is by ill-disguised "Absichten" (intentions) and vulgar simplifications in social relations. Helene is the only character who understands him effortlessly and she does so with the

---

21 H/Wildgans, p. 31.

same intuitive grasp that distinguishes Hans Karl's empathy with his spiritual counterpart, the nonchalant acrobat Furlani. She can say of him to Neuhoff: "Er gehört nur sich selber – niemand kennt ihn, da ist es kein Wunder daß Sie ihn nicht kennen" (LII, 256 He belongs only to himself no one knows him, so it's small wonder that you do not know him). In Act III Scene 8, Hans Karl is moved to say to Helene" "Wie du mich kennst!" Wie du alles weißt" (LII, 301 How you know me, how you seem to know everything!). She has this capacity to understand not just because she is gifted with high intelligence and feminine intuition, but because she possesses a directness devoid of pretense, a truthfulness which places her beyond the reach of irony. All the characters of the comedy are caught up in a web of irony: she alone remains free. Like Chekhov's Sasha in *Ivanov* she has a horror of that pretentious social pastime called "Konversation" and condemns "Worte, die alles wirkliche verflachen und im Geschwätz beruhigen" (LII, 216 words which reduce all that is real and soothe one by mere chitchat). Like Sasha too, she believes in and represents "active love." Antoinette's intuition tells her that Helene *can* only be truthful, even in her facial expression, and Hans Karl recognizes in her an essential truth that belongs to her very being: "in Ihnen liegt das Notwendige" (LII, 261 within you lies the true essence). In creating a figure who is removed from the plane of irony and who represents the uncomplicated self, Hofmannsthal presents us with the perfect foil to his passive hero and a society which thrives on make-believe.

As the very embodiment of social complications, Hans Karl

is an unfailing source of misunderstanding and involuntary embarrassments. Whether he says something or remains mute, he creates confusion; his own and of the society about him. He is the cause that misunderstandings arise in others, not in any active sense, but because the society about him consistently misreads him. They attribute intentions to him where he has none. They seek for subtle meanings where none are to be found. He is presented as the passive hero whose complexities can be seen as social reflexes to the active curiosity and importunity of others. Even his prodigious reputation with the ladies is bound up with his profound resistance to any kind of positive or formal commitment. "Du weißt, ich binde mich so ungern" (LII, 151 You know I don't like binding engagements) he tells Crescence, in terms which signal an ironic meaning beyond their immediate intention. The whole question of his threatened bachelorhood is here implied, as it is in the cautious and ambiguous phrase "ich bin der Helene attachiert" (LII, 151 I am much attached to Helen). These finely contrived ironies of language are a salient feature of Hofmannsthal's comic style and they are wholly appropriate to his reflexive approach to characterization. When Stani observes, "du hast Handgelenk immer geschmeidig, um loszulassen" (LII, 181 You always keep your wrist loose, so that you can let go), he also unwittingly identifies this crucial feature of Hans Karl's nature; the inability to take the initiative or to act decisively. This comic disability reaches its ironic climax in Act III Scene 8, where Helene finds herself slipping into the conventionally male role and barely stops herself from popping the question: "aber das ist doch eine Enormität, daß Sie mich das sagen lassen!" (LII, 299 But really it is quite preposterous that you let me say all this!).

The essential fallibility of language as the flawed vehicle of communication, as the insufficient medium of social intercourse, is Hofmannsthal's preferred preoccupation in *Der Schwierige*. This sophisticated concern with the questionable nature of language in the play, which Alfred Doppler has most helpfully illuminated, is the chief reason why it is so deeply grounded in irony.[22] It may also account for a particular impression one gains from the text; namely that character is conceived and born of language. Here a fine point of distinction may be made with Chekhov's handling of language in the social comedy, for one might appropriately speak of the sporadic occurrence of irony in his dialogue rather than a dominant ironic mode. The sad merry-go-round of hopeless love between characters of *The Seagull* repeatedly produces moments of poignant irony, just as the basic situation of *The Cherry Orchard*, a thriftless family living on in a run-down estate that is to be sold over their heads, is a source of intermittent ironic implication and contrast. Chekhov employs language as a preeminently social and psychological medium, and so for him idiom and tone, mannerism and nuance precisely define the conventions of a particular society in its historical setting. The impulse towards verisimilitude, Chekhov's proverbial "truth to life," remains the dominant.

---

22 Alfred Doppler, "Die Thematisierung der Konversation. Hugo von Hofmannsthals Lustspiel *Der Schwierige*," *Wirklichkeit im Spiegel der Sprache Aufsätze zur Literatur des 20. Jahrhunderts in Österreich*, Vienna: Europa-Verlag, 1975, pp. 65-99.

Irony is not so much the established key, as an irregular intruder in a diversity of linguistic registers and tonalities in which the comic and the serious alternate with the unpredictable rhythm of life itself.

If a comparable figure among Chekhov's passive heroes does exist, then he is to be found in Platonov, a man who is as puzzling to himself as he is to others, and who is introduced in Act I Scene 3 in these terms:

> PORFJRY: Kak vam skazat'? Platonov, po moemu, jest' lutšy vyrazitel' sovremennoi neopredelennostij ... Eto geroi lutsěvo eščě, k sožaleniju, nenapisan- novo, sovremennove romana .... (Smeëtsja). Pod neopredelënnostju ja razumeju sovremennoje sostojanije naševo obšestva: ... On stal v tupik, ter- jaetsja, ne znaet, na čom ostanovitsja, ne ponimajet..., trudno ponjat' ved' etix gospod! (PSS XI, 16)
>
> (How shall I put it? In my view Platonov is the very best example of modern vagueness ... He's the hero of the finest modern novel, alas, as yet unwritten ... (laughs). By vagueness I mean the present state of our society: ... He is at a loss, bewildered, he doesn't know where he stands, he doesn't understand. To be sure, it's hard to understand these gentlemen!)

The "modern vagueness" which he exemplifies points to a wider social and historical representativeness, Platonov, like Hans Karl, is explored through the quizzical eyes of the society around him and these diverse responses, some contradictory, most exaggerated and confused, create about him an air of mystery and complexity. Like Ivanov, who sees himself as "a sort of Hamlet,

Manfred, odd-man-out or the devil knows what" (Act 3 Scene 6), Platonov represents something in the nature of "the modern comic hero" who has lost all direction and purpose in life and whose moral outlook contains few if any certainties. In fact he too is largely innocent of his reputation, and we are brought much closer to the truth about him when he asks: "Čemu ze mešat' –to? Mne ničto ne možet mešat..., ja ležačij karnen. Ležačije kamni sami sozdany dlja tovo, stob ... mešat" (PSS XI, 34 Why be bothered? Nothing can bother me ... I'm an immobile stone. Yet even immobile stone are made to be stumbling blocks). Platonov's inertia or apathy, the cause of so much aggravation, is perhaps his most deep-seated failing and it is one familiar enough in Russian fiction (one has only to recall Oblomov). He is shrewdly assessed by Isaac:

> Ja izučaju vas sovremennix Čackix i ..., ja ponimaju vas! Jesli by vam bylo veselo, jesli by ne bylo tak bezdel'ničeski skučno, to, pover 'te, vy ne trogali by mojevo otca. Vy, gospodin Čackij, ne pravdy isčete, a uveseljaetes', zabavljeates... (PSS XI, 50)

> (I've made a study of your modern day Chatsky's and I understand you only too well! If you were only happy, if you weren't so darned bored and idle, believe me, you wouldn't touch my father. You my dear Mr. Chatsky, are not looking for the truth, but are merely indulging yourself, amusing yourself...)

As an example of the modern misfit, a latter day Chatsky, Platonov's inconsiderate, selfish behavior of course gives offence to all and sundry. In this respect he may be distinguished from the nobler egotism of Hans Karl who observes social proprieties and is discreet to a fault. They are similar chiefly in their social and comic roles as involuntary disturbers of the peace in society, and by virtue of their focal roles they each challenge the standards and attitudes of their social environment.

The institution of marriage is particularly threatened by them, as their amorous entanglements cast them in the role of philanderers, though in the most passive sense conceivable, since it is they who are pursued by women.[23] The havoc wrought by Platonov's reckless adultery certainly takes a more extreme form

---

23 Hans Karl's adventurous affair with Antoinette might, conceivably, have appeared in a much more menacing light in the hands of a playwright with a stronger bias towards social realism, like Shaw for example, or indeed Schnitzler. As a serving officer in the Imperial Austrian Army Graf Bühl would have been subject to the full severities of military law (had he been found out). Paragraph 775 of *Das Militärstrafgesetz Über Verbrechen und Vergehen*, dritte, vollständig umgearbeitete Auflage von Dr. Alexander Koller, Vienna: Taschenausgabe der österreichischen Gestze 23, 1914 reads: "Ehebruch. Strafe. Eine verheiratete Person, die einen Ehebruch begeht, wie auch eine unverheiratete, mit welcher ein Ehebruch begangen wird, ist mit Arrest von einem bis zu sechs Monaten, die Frau aber alsdann strenger zu bestrafen, wenn durch den begangene Ehebruch über die Rechtmäßigkeit der nachfolgenden Geburt ein Zweifel entstehen kann." (Adultery. Penalty. A married person who commits adultery, as well as an unmarried person with whom adultery is committed, is to be punished with one to six months' detention, but then the woman is to be severely punished if, as a result of the adultery, any doubt should arise to the legality of the resultant birth.) On can understand Carl Sternheim's admiring disbelief vis à vis Hans Karl" "Welche Haltung! Lernt man, hat man sie etwas in dem zusammengebrochenen Österreich?" (What bearing! Can such a thing be learnt in an Austria that has collapsed?) Letter to Hofmannsthal, September 1, 1921, HB, 4, 1970, p. 249.

than Hans Karl's anti-marital mischief, which largely belongs to the past anyhow. Whereas Platonov plays fast and loose with the opposite sex, regardless of marriage ('Žnaju ja sebja! Te tol'ko romany i okančivajutsja blagopolučno, v kotoryx menja net„‚") (PSS XI, 104 I know myself! The only love affairs which end happily are those I'm not involved in). Hans Karl sees it as his duty to patch up the marriage between his former mistress Antoinette and the eternal cuckold Hechingen. Platonov invites complications out of an aimless lethargy of the soul devoid of all passion ("Net ničevo vo mne takovo, za što možno bylo by uxvatit'sja net ničevo takovo, za što možno bylo by uvažat' i ljubit.") (PSS XI, 96 There's nothing about me to seize hold of, there's nothing about me to respect or love"), whereas Hans Karl creates confusion through his well-intentioned compliance in serving everyone's interest but his own. Platonov, in typical Chekhovian fashion, attempts a solution by means of escape ("Žavtra ja begu otsjuda, begu ot samovo sebja, sam ne znaju kuda, begu k novoi žyzni!" (PSS XI, 135 Tomorrow I'll escape, escape from myself too, don't quite know where, but I'll escape to a new life!), which culminates in the half-bungled, tragi-comic shooting by Sonya. Hans Karl resolves his difficulties, however provisionally this might be, by drifting into the sanctuary of matrimony.

Wedlock has, for better or worse, been a mainstay of comic theater and has provided it with the convenient and conventional ending. While Chekhov consistently avoided the convention and preferred the hero to make an end of himself, Hofmannsthal was just as surely drawn to it. The trials and vicissitudes of marriage are explored by Chekhov as part of life in all its fallibility, in its tragic, comic or indeed farcical potential, but always with unerring honesty of vision. In Hofmannsthal a heightened moral interest and accentuation attends his treatment of marriage. This match between Hans Karl and Helene is handled with that delicate mixture of playful mysticism and moral seriousness so characteristic of his comic style. Their engagement is never formally sealed but is presented as a *fait accompli* since at the deepest level they had always been of one mind; their marriage has already been sanctioned by Hans Karl's timeless vision ("und sogar das Ja-Wort hab ich gehört") (LII, 265 and I even heard the word 'Yes'"). It is Stani, the categorical simplifier, whose concluding speech throws light on the abiding uncertainty which persists at the formal or social level:

> Was wir heute erlebt haben, war *tant bien que mal*, wenn man's Kind beim Namen nennt, eine Verlobung. Eine Verlobung kulminiert in der Umarmung des verlobten Paares. – In unserem Fall ist das verlobte Paar zu bizarr, um sich an diese Formen zu halten (LII, 314

> (What we have experienced today was, *tant bien que mal*, if you call a spade a spade, a betrothal. A betrothal culminates in an embrace by the betrothed couple. – In our case, the betrothed couple is too bizarre to abide by these formalities.)

Society demands forms to which it can hold, which define and sustain its values and institutions. The happy couple are called "bizarre" because they have dispensed with form; they have preserved the intimacy of their private selves by ignoring the social norm. There is no need for an exchange of rings or an embrace in public since their union has, for them, always existed. Instead it is the best match-maker Crescence who performs the vicarious act by embracing the dumbfounded Altenwyl. The last words of the play "und das Ganze wird sein richtiges, offizielles Gesicht bekommen" (LII, 314 and the whole affair will be given its proper, official look) refer not merely to the need to honor certain social proprieties; they are a tacit reminder of the necessity of form itself as the badge of civilized society. Hofmannsthal no less than Chekhov knew only too well of the fragility of form and of the threat to a society that had lost all sense of it. The comic form, with its subtle ironies, provided a perfect vehicle for mirroring the threatened fabric of contemporary social reality. Form itself had become problematical. As Hofmannsthal's paradoxical aphorism points out: "Die Formen beleben und töten" (A, 47 Forms enliven and deaden).

Hofmannsthal and Oscar Wilde*

Wer die Schönheit angeschaut mit Augen,
Ist dem Tode schon anheimgegeben
—August von Platen

On ne peut juger de la beauté de
la vie que par celle de la mort
—Comte de Lautreamont

The relative neglect and underestimation of Oscar Wilde by the English is something that tends to puzzle Continentals, for this radical prophet of new aesthetic creed has been more honored abroad than at home. In France, Russia or Germany, he has always been an acknowledged literary force, far more widely regarded, for instance, than his fellow-Irishman Bernard Shaw. Perhaps today, after the publication of Richard Ellmann's magnificent biography of Wilde in 1987, there are signs of a turning point. Ellmann's meticulous, scholarly, and highly readable work,

---

* Editions of Oscar Wilde's writings to (with abbreviations in bracket): Oscar Wilde, *The Picture of Dorian Gray*, ed. Robert B. Ross, Paris: Carrington, 1908 OW I; *The Artist as Critic*, London: Allen, 1970 OW II, *Reviews*, ed. Robert B. Ross, London: Methuen, 1908 OW III; *Letters of Oscar Wilde*, ed. Rupert Hart-Davis, London: Hart-Davis, 1962, Letters of OW.

is fitted to usher in a proper revaluation of the writer, for we now have a far more differentiated and refined picture of the originality of mind that could fascinate, challenge and entertain a host of the distinguished contemporaries. What he writes of Wilde's influence on Gide, may also be seen as relevant to his wider European significance:

> What Wilde provided for Gide, at a crucial moment of the latter's youth, was a way of extricating himself from an aestheticism which had not yet come to grips with love, religion, or life, and from a religion which offered safety only at the cost of being perpetually on guard. He did this not by rejecting aesthetics or ethics, but by turning sacred things out to make them sacred. He showed souls becoming carnal and lusts becoming spiritual. He showed the aesthetic world not isolated from experience, but infused into it. This was the new Hellenism of which he liked to speak.[1]

The aesthetic movement of the late nineteenth century, which attracted so many of the notable artists and writers of the day, including Hofmannsthal, was much more than an extravagant cult or a passing fashion. It was a deeply felt and serious challenge to the sterile utilitarian values of a shallow materialist age. These conflicts were all involved in nurturing a new aesthetic awareness. As poet, theorist, celebrity and wit, Wilde represented the focal point of this highly self-conscious, proselytizing movement. It is not surprising, then, that the highly impressionable young Hofmannsthal fell under the spell of this "Apostle of Beauty,"

---

1 Richard Ellmann, *Oscar Wilde*, London: Hamilton, 1987, p. 340.

as a contemporary critic called him.[2] In a strictly limited sense,

---

[2] "Der Apostel der Schönheit," a phrase used by "Erinnerungen an Oscar Wilde," NDR, 1903, p. 307. In his pioneering essay, "Hofmannsthals Wandlung," in *Über Hugo von Hofmansthal*, Göttingen: Vandenhoeck & Ruprecht, 1948, pp. 142-160, Richard Alewyn has shown how *Das Märchen der 672. Nacht* may be seen to have foreshadowed Wilde's destiny as the epitome of the age of aestheticism. He has, however, omitted to investigate Wilde's own creation, Dorian Gray, as the very type of the aesthete and the specifically literary influence which Wilde's work exerted on Hofmannsthal. R. Breugelmanns, "Oscar Wilde und Hugo von Hofmannsthal: Ein Vergleich im Zusammenhang Ihrer geistesgeschichtlichen Zeitlage," in *Proceedings of the 14th Annual Meeting of the Pacific Northwest Conference on Foreign Languages*, ed. Roger Motut and E. Maxheimer, Banff: typescript, 1963, pp. 184-197, deals too emphatically and without differentiation with what are pointed to as evident affinities between the writers in thematic and stylistic treatment. The only work properly considered is *Elektra* where similarities are, and have always been, evident. Without critical tact and discrimination, many of the parallels drawn are unconvincing. Eugene Weber, "Hofmannsthal und Oscar Wilde," HF vol. 1, Freiburg: Hofmannsthal Gesellschaft, 1971, pp. 99-106 is more careful and selective in approach. In what is largely a commentary on the essay "Sebastian Melmoth" he too stresses Hofmannsthal's "Begeisterung für Oscar Wilde" (enthusiasm for Oscar Wilde) as generally valid and yet takes too little account of Hofmannsthal's changing relationship, which involved critical detachment. Margaret Jacobs, in her edition *Hugo von Hofmannsthal Four Stories*, Oxford: Oxford University Press, 1968, pp. 27 f, builds on Alewyn's discussion of the *Märchen* in relation to Wilde by stressing rather the "unconscious insult" to reality in the Kaufmannssohn's docile passivity by contrast to Wilde's "deliberate insulting of reality." Aatos Ojala, *Aestheticism and Oscar Wilde*, Helsinki: Suomaleinen Tiedeakat, 1954, provides a thorough and illuminating account of Wilde's aestheticist theory and practice yet makes no reference to Hofmannsthal (a sad reflection on the latter's standing in English studies which, even today, has little changed). Guido Glur, "Kunstlehre und Kunstanschauung des Georgekreises und die Ästhetik Oscar Wildes," *Sprache und Dichtung*,

Hofmannsthal's early work does show traces of Wilde's influence, yet one does well to resist pursuing isolated literary echoes and stylistic similarities, since they are so finely interfused with those of other writers as to make selection precarious. Instead, it seems more fruitful to dwell on only a few prominent examples which appear particularly revealing. It will, therefore, be my primary purpose to draw attention to certain distinct contrasts between these two writers, born almost exactly twenty years apart, both in conceptual terms and in those of formal treatment. The points of contact essentially belong to Hofmannsthal's early years and appear to be unimportant after *Elektra* (1903). By the time he came to write his essay on Wilde in 1905, Hofmannsthal had entered a new phase of wider creativity and was able to survey his subject as a phenomenon of the past with detachment and estranged fascination.

The early Hofmannsthal shows an affinity with Wilde not merely in a formal sense by a certain congruence of style, but in a subtler way, through a number of kindred sympathies, by the choice of subject, and the use of motifs. The range of their writing

---

Neue Folge 3, 1957, pp. 3-112 takes some account of Hofmannsthal in discussing Wilde's theories (pp. 26-31 et passim) but does not enter into the problem of literary relations. Wolfdietrich Rasch's article "Claudio: Zur Darstellung der Lebensferne in der Dichtung um 1900," in *Jahrbuch der deutschen Schillergesellschaft*, vol. 22, 1978, pp. 552-571, traces persistently recurring features of the sophisticated, weak-willed hero (termed by him "der Lebensflüchtling – the refugee from life) who abounds in the writing of that time and who stands in varying degrees of proximity to Hofmannsthal's Claudio. It is surprising to find no mention of Dorian Gray in his panoramic survey of European Decadence.

also shows a distinct parallelism. Both first realized their gifts as lyrical poets (though Wilde possesses a degree of artifice and intellectuality which mars even his best verse); both were essayists of the first order and used the form liberally to include the dialogue, the public address and the review on a similar range of topics; both commanded the tragedy as well as the social comedy (though in the drama Hofmannsthal's range and compass are pre-eminent); both were strongly attracted to the allegorical fairytale and short story; both wrote one novel in a highly personal, self-exploratory vein; both published collections of sayings and aphorisms. Though a few of these affinities are explored, comparison will generally yield to contrast. Hofmannsthal's entire literary development was altogether more embracing and diverse indeed, it was more European for it was sustained by an increasing awareness of the importance of handing on the extinguishing torch of tradition. His creative purpose and endeavor thus has dimensions that were denied Wilde, who died in 1900 before those cataclysms broke loose which shook the very foundations of a culture and lent urgency to Hofmannsthal's "creative restoration." His impressive activities as editor and anthologist alone (this includes *Deutsche Erzähler,* 1912; *Österreichische Bibliothek,* 1915 ff; *Rodauner Nachträge,* 1918; *Wort und Ehre deutscher Sprache,* 1927 *German writers of Fiction, Austrian Library, Rodaun Supplements, The Arabian Nights, German Reader, Value and Distinction of the German Language*) are ample illustration of that will to revive and nurture literary values, to hand on the best of what the past has produced before it is buried and forgotten. To place the work of the two writers side by side, or to recognize in Hofmannsthal the richer store of forms and the more catholic range of interests. They are comparable too in their high degree of self-awareness as writers, though in Hofmannsthal we can see a more distinctive and diversified artistic development as he crosses the threshold of Modernism. However, Wilde remains the more emphatic creative personality; one who commands more striking effects and makes more immediate impact on the world about him.

In his life and works Wilde was, for most, the chief figure of aestheticism, a living embodiment of the movement; he was the very paragon of the artist wholly dedicated to beauty, a champion of individualism who had raised the creative personality to the highest principle of life. Beyond that, he was one who waged an incessant polemic against cultural philistinism and who challenged the basic assumptions of Victorian morality.[3] This conscious assimilation of the foremost trends of the age within the personality may make comparison with Friedrich Nietzsche superficially attractive, and Thomas Mann was once tempted to claim that many of Wilde's sayings might be attributed to the philosopher, just as several aphorisms by Nietzsche might well be found in Wilde's comedies.[4] Yet this judgment appears rather

---

3 "Oscar Wilde on the Witness Stand" in OW II, pp. 435-438. Several passages in *Dorian Gray* are significant also, especially that in which Lord Henry opens to Dorian the prospect of the corruptness of the Victorian age are on pages 67, 124, 296, 314.

4 Thomas Mann, "Nietzsches Philosophie im Lichte unserer Erfahrung," *Das Essayistische Werk Schriften und Reden zur Literatur, Kunst und Philosophie*, vol. 3, Fischer Bücherei, Frankfurt am Main: Fischer, 1968,

facile once the distinctions in tone, function and import of these, so often willful, paradoxes are properly weighed; and Mann betrays his critical malaise by admitting to a sense of sacrilege at identifying Nietzsche, that "Heiliger des Immoralismus" (Saint of Immoralism), with the dandified, whimsical and less saintly Wilde. What is interesting in Mann's linking of the two names is that it reveals a different level of response to Wilde, for in Germany he has always evoked a degree of critical seriousness and philosophical interest which he was not accustomed to receive in England, where he was consistently scourged in the pages of *Punch* or ridiculed to the music of Gilbert and Sullivan's *Patience*.

This qualitative difference in the reception of Wilde on the Continent as a whole, and in Germany in particular, is well attested by the appearance of a *Wilde-Brevier* (*Wilde Handbook*) in 1904 from his publishers, J. J. C. Brun's Verlag, Minden Westphalia.[5] It is hardly conceivable that such a publication containing Wilde's recorded sayings, under the solemn headings, "Die Kunst, Die Kritik, Der Mensch, Die Gesellschaft, Die Moral" (Art, Criticism, Man, Society, Morality), could have been offered to the British public within a few years of his death. The editor of these assorted paradoxes, aperçus, and *bon-mots* has attempted to organize Wilde's ideas "nach inneren Gesichtspunkten" (according to inner points of view) so that they appear as parts of a coherent

---

pp. 33 f.
5 Lawrence M. Price, *The Reception of English Literature in Germany*, New York and London: Blom, 1968, p. 441, who reports, "Oscar Wilde was, even before the war, better known in Germany than in his own country,"

whole. The very attempt is misplaced seriousness, for it doggedly pursues the search for a consistent Weltanschauung in this contradictory mind and fails to distinguish between contexts and levels of utterance, bestowing like emphasis on every trifle. The status accorded to Wilde was predominantly that of an eloquent spokesman of culture, a civilizing influence in a shallow and pretentious age. Once translated and ordered, Wilde's words seemed, in some subtle manner, to take on a note of authority which was perhaps authenticated by his courageous public persona. The attention and respect he commanded at the turn of the century was certainly beyond question. A German reviewer of *The Picture of Dorian Gray* wrote in 1904: "jetzt sind wir von einer Oscar Wilde Epidemie heimgesucht" (We have now been struck by an Oscar Wilde epidemic).[6]

Wilde himself was astutely conscious of the representative nature of his role as a man of letters. In that famous missive to Lord Alfred Douglas known as *De Profundis* he writes:

> I was a man who stood in symbolic relations to the art and culture of my age. I had realized this for myself at the very dawn of my manhood, and had forced my age to realize it afterwards. Few men hold such a position in their own lifetime, and have it so acknowledged.[7]

This proud sense of selfhood and mission informs even the work of contrite humility. The paradox of his nature is such that he can be both the accuser of his age and its victim, stand in

---

6 anon., *Die neue Rundschau*, vol. 15, 1904, p. 381. 7, 8
7 OW Letters, p. 466.

judgment of his failings and vices and fall prey to its allurements. In the same letter he confesses:

> I would sooner say or hear it said of me, that I was so typical a child of my age, that in my perversity, and for that perversity's sake, I turned the good things of my life to evil, and the evil things of my life to good.[8]

That consciousness of belonging to the intellectual temper of an age is clearly present, though far less committed, in the young Hofmannsthal, and so the question of common good among writers of the time – of shared preoccupations, similarities of aesthetic response, affinities in style – is virtually impossible to isolate and treat in terms of a particular literary influence. Hofmannsthal was wont to generalize with deft suggestiveness about the common cultural legacy shared by his generation, "den Spätgeborenen" (PI, 147 those born late), an international community of sophisticated youth distinguished by their refined sense of beauty and extreme sensibility (PI, 148).[9] The cultural ties and kindred sensibilities "dieser geistigen Freimaurerei" (this intellectual freemasonry) dispersed among the major cities of Europe, created, as he sensed, an easy ambiance, an intuitive understanding. The high degree of consciousness, even in the

---

8 OW Letters, p. 469.
9 Hofmannsthal's letter of December 19, 1892 to K. A. Klein is an indication of his earlier sense of affinity with Wilde and other near-contemporaries: "Ich werde übrigens nächstens versuchen, in Tagesblättern die uns verwandten Erscheinungen fremder Literaturen (Verlaine, Swinburne, Oscar Wilde, die Praeraphaeliten etc.) zu besprechen" (Incidentally I shall soon attempt to review those figures in foreign literatures which are similar to us [Verlaine etc.]).

early Hofmannsthal, of the perils of aestheticism has not always been fully recognized. The essays on Swinburne, d'Annunzio and Pater, all published under the name "Loris," give evidence of intellectual detachment, perspicacity and critical reservation vis-à-vis aestheticism as a mode of thought and perception.[10] It rests, we are told, on a conception of beauty which is sterile and lifeless: "der Schönheit an sich, der moralfremden, zweckfremden, lebenfremden" (Pl, 99 beauty *per se* is alien to morality, to purpose, to life); it is termed "gefährlich wie Opium" (Pl, 204 dangerous as opium) and deemed deficient in relation to the fullness and splendor of life: Hofmannsthal speaks of "die Unzulänglichkeit des Ästhetizismus" (the insufficiency of aestheticism) whose charm lies in "Nebensachen" (Pl, 205 peripheral things). He writes disparagingly of "einer morbiden Narcissus-Schönheit" (Pl, 205 a morbid narcissus-beauty) as characteristic of the moment, which seeks for beauty everywhere, even in "der Schönheit des Sterbens,

---

10   This critical independence is perhaps best exemplified by Hofmannsthal's perplexed diary entry of October 10, 1906 (A, 152) which takes issue with the persistent misunderstanding of his early work: "Sonderbarer endlos wiederholter Vorwurf meinen ersten Produkten gegenüber, daß sie aus einer egoistischen ästhetischen Einsamkeit, einer unmenschlichen, der Sympathie baren Natur hervorgehen. In *Gestern* und *Tor und Tod* handelt as sich eben gerade um das Finden eines höheren Verhältnisses zu den Menschen. Man muß diese Gedichte so oberflächlich als möglich auffassen, um das nicht herauszufühlen" (Strange, endlessly repeated charge against my first products, that they spring from an egotistical, aesthetic solitude, an inhumane nature devoid of sympathy. In *Yesterday* and *Death and the Fool* it is the question of the discovery of a higher relationship toward human beings. One has to regard these poems as superficially as possible not to gain a sense of this).

des Totseins" (the beauty of dying, being dead). He further notes in his diary in June 1894: "Oscar Wilde 'Intentions': starker narkotischer Zauber, sophistisch verführerisch" (A, 108 strong narcotic enchantment, sophistically seductive). The associations of a narcotic effect which drowns the critical faculties, a seductiveness of language which charms sensibility and imprisons the mind, recur in the poem *Der Prophet*.

> Ein Zaubertrunk hält jeden Sinn befangen
> Und alles flüchtet hilflos, ohne Halt
>
> (A magic potion holds every sense in bondage
> And all flees helplessly and without stay)

And:

> Von seinen Worten, den unscheinbar leisen
> Geht eine Herrschaft aus und ein Verführen,
> Er macht die leere Luft beengend kreisen
> Und er kann töten ohne zu berühren (A, 94, 95)
>
> (Out of his words, so innocently gentle
> There flows a magisterial seductive power,
> He makes the empty air oppressive in its turning
> And can kill without the slightest touch.)

Although this poem attempts to frame in words his uneasy relationship to Stefan George, it moves within precisely the same conceptual and intuitive range as the notes on Wilde. It expresses a recoiling of the mind before a threat to its freedom, the fear of the irresistible enchantment of words, that fascination with the power of beauty which has the touch of death. Preoccupation with the theme of death and a complementary fascination for the experimental attitude to life are together part of the climate of the *fin-de siècle* and a trait shared by Wilde and the young Hofmannsthal. The age's dalliance with death and evil reveals an avidness for strong emotion and novelty of experience which in Wilde's art, where it is pronounced, readily leads to exoticism, to a level of artificiality which is too fastidious. In Hofmannsthal, death is more than a dark ornament of life. Though death still appears remote, uncanny and inaccessible to the poet of *Der Jüngling und die Spinne* (*The Youth and the Spider*) and *Idylle* (Idyll), it assumes a palpable presence in *Der Tor und der Tod*, in *Jedermann* and *Das Salzburger große Welttheater* (*Death and the Fool, Everyman, The Salzburg Great World Theater*). This plasticity and force is, in large measure, due to Hofmannsthal's decided turn towards traditional forms such as the mystery play and the *theatrum mundi*. But he also commands a deeper seriousness of treatment which springs from an ethical accentuation which remains characteristic of him.

Hofmannsthal comes closest to Wilde in two depictions of the figure of the aesthete (Claudio and the "Kaufmannssohn" merchant's son), and in that powerful dance of death, *Elektra*.[11] I shall limit myself to the earliest of these works. Two conflicting forms of inward response are poetically evoked in *Der Tor und der Tod*: a haunting sensuous allurement and a dread of the illusory life

---

11 In *Ad me ipsum* (A, 215) Hofmannsthal wrote: "Die Bedeutung des Namens Claudio für den *Toren* (von *claudere*)" (The significance of the name Claudio for the *Fool* [from *claudere*]), The Latin verb means to limp or to be lame and, by extension, to halt, waver, be defective. Figuratively, therefore, it suggests Claudio's moral disabilities.

devoid of feeling and deathlike in its emptiness. This ambivalence of attraction and aversion is embodied in the figure of Death, who is introduced to the sweet strains of a violin which addresses Claudio's soul: "Musik? Und seltsam zu der Seele redend" (GLD, 277 Music? and strangely to the soul expressive). The key elements of this conception, and indeed much of the atmosphere of the work, owe a good deal to *The Picture of Dorian Gray*. To read the two works side by side is to notice many thematic and motivic similarities.[12] The portrayal of the solitary youthful figure in his mansion, attended by an old manservant, surrounded by decorous beauty, stylish furniture and precious *objets d'art*, shows clear resemblances. Above all, the inner psychological dimension, the atmospheric coloring in the treatment of the hollow narcissist existence are closely related. Hofmannsthal's symbolic representation of the three closest human bonds through the figures of the mother, the lover and the friend also find their correspondence in Dorian Gray's callous relationships to his family, Sibyl Vane and Basil Hallward. For Dorian, that symbol of the new hedonism, Death is also personified in the mind as he remembers the love he willfully destroyed: "She had often mimicked death on the stage. Then Death himself had touched her, and taken her with him"

---

12 To illustrate the strong thematic parallelism, certain formulations in Dorian Gray are converted into crucial motifs in *Der Tor und der Tod*: e. g. "To become the spectator of one's own life as Harry says is to escape the suffering of life" (p. 124); "the whole book seemed to him to contain the story of his own life, written before he had lived it" (p. 143) "Life had become too hideous a burden for him to bear" (p. 228) "It was the living death of his own soul that troubled him: (p. 245).

(OW I, 118). The immediate connection between contemplation of death and the making of a moral choice is equally present in both works. Death introduces himself to Claudio as "ein großer Gott der Seele" (a mighty god of the soul) and by this phrase fashions a link between the aesthetic and the moral, for by his appearance the questionable issue of Claudio's life is laid bare. Hofmannsthal had noted in his diary in 1893, the year in which *Der Tor und der Tod* appeared: "Die Grundlage des Ästhetischen ist Sittlichkeit" (A, 101 Morality is the foundation of the aesthetics). Moreover, his essay, "Der neue Roman von D'Annunzio" ("D'Annunzio's new novel") introduces "das Principium der sittlichen Schönheit" (the principle of moral beauty) as a recognizable immanent category in literature (Pl, 239f). It is also noteworthy that Wilde uses the expression "the ethical beauty of the story" in referring to his novel.[13]

Hofmannsthal's figure Death uses deeply sensuous words which mirror that aesthetic self-indulgence, that hedonism which denies all but its own satisfaction. It is the seductive voice of aestheticism which addresses Claudio:

> In jeder wahrhaft großen Stunde,
> Die schauern deine Erdenform gemacht,
> Hab ich dich angerührt im Seelengrunde
> Mit heiliger, geheimnisvoller Macht (GLD, 280)

---

13 Letters of OW, p. 269. This statement is an apparent contradiction of Wilde's reiterated views about the separateness of ethics and aesthetics. (Cf. note 14 below). Here he is affirming "ethical import" as merely part of the work's expressiveness and an aspect registered by those who have no real receptivity for style.

(At every truly fateful moment
Which deeply shook your mortal frame,
I touched you in your soul's foundation
With sacred and mysterious power).

Death's mission is to rouse a moral awareness which is noted in the soul. The breadth of meaning both Hofmannsthal and Wilde attribute to the term "soul" may fluctuate according to the context, but it is a word that occurs constantly throughout their respective writings and assuredly has reference to man's deepest self, to his spiritual being. That each of them is also touching on a moral problem in writing of a destructiveness of a life dedicated to a narcissist philosophy, seems to me beyond question. Yet there remained uncertainty in the reception of Dorian Gray. Wilde's avowals as to "the extremely obvious moral" or again, "a terrible moral" in the novel merely show up its inherent ambiguity and the need for subsequent apologetics.[14] Hofmannsthal's Claudio,

---

14 This is oddly at variance with the famous preface to the novel in which he categorically states: "There is no such thing as a moral or an immoral book. Books are well written or badly written. That is all," And again: "No artist has ethical sympathies. All ethical sympathy in an artist is an unpardonable mannerism of style." Gilbert in *The Critic as Artist* pronounces: "All art is immoral" (OW II, 380) and "the sphere of ethics are absolutely distinct and separate" (OW II, 393). See also Letters of OW pp. 263f., and 159f., where he admits that his novel is "far too crowded with sensational detail and far too paradoxical in style." Everywhere he affirms his autobiographical aspect: "it contains much of me in it. Basil Hallward is what I think I am: Lord Henry what the world thinks of me: Dorian Gray what I would like to be – in other ages perhaps." This wavering between moral censure and self-identification is all too apparent in the shifting perspectives of Wilde's narrative style. For a balanced scholarly treatment of Wilde's aesthetics cf. Leonard A.

though condemned in the very title, also displays a degree of empathy for the beautiful life which is too easily interpreted as acquiescence.[15]

Not just the theme of death, but language and imaginative range link *Salome* and *Elektra* by some striking affinities, as was recognized by critics from the start. Alfred Kerr, in reviewing Hofmannsthal's early development as dramatist in 1905, juxtaposed the two plays and drew attention to the animal ferocity and ecstatic sensualism which they shared.[16] The sophisticated

---

Willoughby, "Oscar Wilde and Goethe The Life of Art and the Art of Life," PEGS 35, 1965, pp. 1-37.

15 I cannot agree with Wolfdietrich Rasch's somewhat equivocal view of Claudio as a figure who appears to stand in some sense beyond good and evil. Rasch writes (op. cit., p. 565): "Claudios Verhalten ist gewiß ohne moralischen Wert, aber deshalb doch nicht schuldhaft, sondern jenseits der sittlichen Kategorien, gewissermaßen praemoralisch. (Claudios attitude is certainly without moral value yet still not culpable, but rather beyond moral categories, in a sense pre-moral). This seems to me to overlook some of the formal and traditional elements of the work which clearly derive from the morality play as well as to ignore Hofmannsthal's own avowed ethical accentuations, however unobtrusively introduced.

16 Alfred Kerr, *Das neue Drama*, Berlin: Fischer, 1905, p. 102: "die Elektra von Hofmannsthal ist ein Rachetier: wie etwa Jochanan bei Oscar Wilde ein Verzückungstier ist" (Hofmannsthal's *Elektra* is a beast of vengeance: just as Jochanan in Oscar Wilde is a beast of ecstasy). Typical of the sense of closeness in association between the plays is the request by Henry Graf Kessler that Hofmannsthal should write a ballet sequence for the dancer Ruth St. Denis who was to perform Salome in Berlin in 1906. Cf. *Hugo von Hofmannsthal-Harry Graf Kessler Briefwechsel, 1898-1929*, ed. Hilde Burger, Frankfurt am Main: Fischer, 1968, p. 79. Hofmannsthal did not, in the event, comply. For further contemporary critics' responses to *Salome* and *Elektra* cf. *Hofmannsthal*

primitivism of these two plays, their powerful rhetorical styles, their glowing carnal imagery and the importance to both of the culminating symbol of the dance as myth and ritual, all bring about an obviously close parallelism. What Kerr called "das Geschmacklerische" (the fussiness of taste) in Hofmannsthal, or similarly, "verinnerlichte Stilkunst" (internalized artistry of style), he had also detected in Wilde in an earlier review (1903). There he asks "Was ist der Kern von Oscar Wilde? Oscar Wilde ist ein Stilkünstler. Sehr zweifelhaft ob er mehr ist. " (What is at the core of Oscar Wilde? Oscar Wilde is an artist of style. It is most doubtful if he is anything more).[17] Kerr's strong reservations as to the content of Wilde's art seem to set the stamp of formalism upon it. Yet this response is significantly qualified, Wilde is to Kerr, "ein Herausholer des wesentlichen Moments; ein starker Kyrstallisator," in short, "Wilde stylisiert" (a picker-out of the essential element; a strong crystallizer).[18] Since this category of stylization is equally applied by Kerr to the early Hofmannsthal, we must judge how far the awareness of period style overrides, indeed clouds individual appreciation of their art. Such critical response is perfectly defensible, especially in a contemporary critic, yet distinctions are to be made; for in Hofmannsthal an individual style becomes increasingly important, as we shall see.

Wilde, in reviewing Swinburne's poetry, states: "he is so

---

im Urteil seiner Kritiker, Gotthard Wunberg ed., Frankfurt am Main: Athenäum, 1972, pp. 160, 258.
17 Alfred Kerr, p. 280
18 Alfred Kerr, p. 281.

eloquent that everything he touches becomes unreal."[19] It is a judgment that would fit his own style equally well, for eloquence is not a temptation which Wilde himself could resist. On the contrary; he was forever championing the ascendancy of formal beauty over content and idea, claiming that "the artist is the creator of beautiful things,"[20] that "Beauty reveals everything, because it expresses nothing," that "all bad poetry springs from genuine feeling." [21] And yet one can tax Wilde quite justifiably for falling in to mannerism as well as sentimentality, for both belong to an age in which his sensibilities were formed. There are passages in Dorian Gray which do not express the subtle beauty he had hoped to evoke. The precious artificiality of period taste is clearly reflected in such sentences as: "in the grass, white daisies were tremulous"; "a rose shook in her blood, and shadowed her cheeks. Quick breath parted the petal of her lips"; "She trembled all over and shook like a white narcissus."[22] This is period style indeed, the mirror of a fashionable taste at the *fin-de-siècle*. Wilde's decorous language is sometimes overcome by the burden of its ostentatiousness and flounders into fragrant *Kitsch*. There is no point of comparison here with Hofmannsthal's narrative prose, with the style of *Andreas* for instance, which is all lucidity, gracefulness and simplicity; displaying the difficult art of restraint, as he himself noted: "Es liegt ein Geheimnis des hohen Stils in dem,

---

19 OW III, p. 520.
20 Preface to Dorian Gray (OW I, ix).
21 OW II, pp. 368, 398.
22 OW I, pp. 7, 96, 121.

was nicht erwähnt wird. (A, 199 A certain mystery of elevated style lies in that which is not mentioned). In Wilde's fairy tales and prose poems one is often alienated by the pretentiousness of manner, the cultivated polish, the use of remote or biblical vocabulary with over-anxious solicitude. This style displays too great a desire to please and succeeds in pleasing too little. Hofmannsthal described this trend in English letters between 1860 and 1890 as "zu scharfes Auseinandergehen, paradox und verdorben" (A, 123 too sharp a separation, paradoxical and corrupted). The essays, on the other hand, show Wilde's controlled eloquence and occupy as significant a position in his writings as do Hofmannsthal's within his. Nevertheless, Hofmannsthal found Wilde's collection of essays, *Intentions*, which includes some of his best prose "unelegant paradoxal" (A, 108 inelegantly paradoxical).

The idea that one critical attitude is as plausible as another, provided that it is verbally appealing, sophisticated and consistent, is argued in Wilde's brilliant essay "The Truth of Masks." This ends with the declaration that there is much in his essay with which he entirely disagrees. That is a frivolous standpoint Hofmannsthal would have disowned. Questions of aesthetic judgment were not for him a matter of such relative, interchangeable values. In his notes on *Der Kaiser und die Hexe* (*The Emperor and the Witch*) Hofmannsthal speculates on the literary flaw of "ein Zuviel im Reden, ein Übertreiben" (a surfeit in speaking, exaggeration), and sees in this the danger (one all too familiar in his early phase) of obliterating the distinction between imagination and truth: "Ein Verwischen der Grenze zwischen Phantasie und Wirklichkeit, also Lüge" (A, 230f a blurring of the boundary between imagination and truth, falsehood). For Hofmannsthal increasingly sees language as a social vehicle of communication with binding values, and Wilde's use of paradox was often a mere plaything, not the instrument of deeper ethical discernment. As a form it fits Wilde's temperament perfectly: it is the mask behind which his contentious self could hide. Unlike the more complex, intuitive form of the aphorism, to which Hofmannsthal was devoted, Wilde's paradoxes display bold contrivance and verbal artifice and as such they blend perfectly into the texture of his comedies.

Distinctions are more important than affinities between Wilde and Hofmannsthal as comic playwrights. In a late essay, Hofmannsthal draws an analogy between the Restoration comedy and that of Wilde and Noel Coward. These modern descendants are seen as "nicht weniger geistreich-frivol, ihre Figuren nicht weniger elegant und reizvoll (bei äußerster Herzenskälte)" (no less witty and volatile, their figures no less elegant and charming [for all their extreme aloofness]).[23] The identification of an imperturbable *sang-froid*, that cold snobbery of tone which treats all topics with the same frivolous wit, greatly contrasts with his own dramatic practice. Hofmannsthal did not learn his technique from Wilde, for he commands an infinite range of tonalities in his comic dialogues and uses subtle counterpoint to play one voice off against another. While Wilde's characters carefully attune their manner

---

23 "Das Publikum der Salzburger Festspiele" P IV, 468f. (The Publication of the Salzburg Festival).

and idiom to the tone appropriate to society, Hofmannsthal differentiates tone according to situation and speaker. The effort to develop a finely expressive individual style is most consciously pursued after "Ein Brief" of 1902. In a revealing diary entry of 1904 he notes: "richtig das Bestreben nach individuellem Stil zu begreifen als die einzige Möglichkeit, sich ewig zu fühlen" (A, 139 correct: to understand the striving for an individual style as the sole means of feeling timeless). His mature development and his many searching and subtle essays on language fully confirm this conviction.

Hofmannsthal's essay "Sebastian Melmoth" (the name Wilde used after his release from Reading Gaol) appeared in the same year as *De Profundis* and clearly shows in reference and allusion the impact of that soul-searching letter.[24] Hofmannsthal offers

---

24 Hofmannsthal's essay first appeared in *Der Tag*, Berlin on March 9, 1905. *De Produndis* was published in a translation by Max Meyerfeld ["De Profundis Aufzeivchnungen und Briefe aus dem Zuchthaus in Reading"] in the *Neue Deutsche Rundschau XVIter Jahrgang der freien Bühne*, vol. 1, January 1905, pp. 86-104, 163-191. This actually preceded the English version first published by Methuen & Co. in February 1905. Kessler sent Hofmannsthal a copy of the English text on March 9, 1905, having just read his essay on Wilde. These early versions of *De Profundis* in fact contained less than half the letter. The full text was suppressed by Robert Ross and published for the first time in 1950 (cf. Letters of OW, pp. 423-511). Hofmannsthal's essay opens with a reference to the mask, an image often found in Wilde, and also alludes to classical motifs (Bacchus, Oedipus, the Sphinx), which figure prominently in Wilde's writing. One sentence might serve as a summary of Dorian Gray's existence: "Oscar Wilde glänzte, entzückte, verletzte, verführte, verriet und wurde verraten, stach ins Herz und wurde ins Herz gestochen" (PH 116 Oscar Wilde scintillated, delighted, offended, betrayed

an inner portrait, a penetrating study of the writer's personality heightened into symbolic dimensions. The aptness of metaphor, deriving largely from Wilde's writings, shows a profound familiarity with his subject. The tragic and the banal are presented as the crucial aspects of Wilde's "Wesen und Schicksal" (being and fate); an insight uncannily prefigured by the work itself. Wilde in retrospect summarized the contradiction of his life in a bitter paradox: "I treated art as the supreme reality and life as a mere mode of fiction."[25] This finds its answer in Hofmannsthal's essay "Man darf nicht alles sondern. Es ist alles überall. Es ist Tragisches in den oberflächlichen Dingen und Albernes in den tragischen" (PII, 119 One must not separate everything. All things exist in all places. There is something tragic in superficial things and banality in tragic things). Hofmannsthal's work (especially *Das Märchen der 672. Nacht, The Tale of the 672nd Night*) always affirms the mysterious and inescapable connectedness between the ugly, the sordid and the beautiful: it resists the unresolved paradox as a mark of existence through the power of form which overcomes the dislocations of life, As he himself succinctly put it:

---

and was betrayed, stabbed to the heart and was stabbed to the heart). The striking metaphor in another sentence is equally derivative: "Und er fühlte wie das Leben sich duckte, ihn aus dem Dunkel anzuspringen" (And he felt how life crouched so as to spring at him from the darkness). This echoes Dorian Gray as he muses uneasily on his new hedonistic life: "In black fantastic shape, dumb shadows crawl into corners of the room, and crouch there" (OW I, 147). Hofmannsthal evidently read Wilde extensively in the original and shows intimate knowledge of the range of his work.
25 Letters of OW, p. 466.

Form als Erhaltende; Welt=in Formen gefangenes; gerettetes Chaos (A, 127)

(Form, the sustaining principle; World=chaos captured in and saved by form).

The Poet and His Public.
Hofmannsthal's "Ideal Listener"

Welchen Leser ich wünsche? Den unbefangensten, der mich,
  Sich und die Welt vergißt, und in dem Buche nur lebt.

—Goethe, Vier Jahreszeiten

In the last of his "Drei kleine Betrachtungen" (1912 *Three little Studies*) entitled "Schöne Sprache" ("Beautiful Diction") Hofmannsthal reflects on a number of issues connected with language which had profoundly occupied him throughout his life: on the question of style, on the relationship of formal expression to "Gehalt" (import) and more particularly on the connection – a necessary one as he saw it – between the creative use of language and its recipient, the listener or reader (for practical purposes the terms "Zuhörer" and "Leser" – listener and reader – are here employed synonymously).[1] This late essay which concerns itself with prose style bears the stamp of that patient thoroughness, that subtle moderation in abstract discourse which characterizes the mature prose. Hofmannsthal is here concerned to explore the connection between the writer and his product, between personality and style. He uses Montaigne's formulation "tel par la

---

1 This chapter is a revised and modified version of a paper read at the Institute of Germanic Studies on May 3, 1979 in commemoration of the fiftieth anniversary of Hofmannsthal's death.

bouche que sur le papier" (by spoken no less than by written word) to establish for the writer the image of a mouth that speaks and accentuates; the written word thus becomes a living utterance, "eine Art von versteckter Mündlichkeit" (a kind of covert oral means) which addresses an envisaged reader. This inheritance of a living voice in the work of accomplished prose ("das schön geschriebene Buch" – the well-written book – is the phrase used for convenience) is raised to a principle of all fine style: "somit ist alles Geschriebene ein Zwiegespräch und keine einfache Äußerung" (PIV, 52 thus everything written is a dialogue, and no mere utterance). Writing is therefore creative in a twofold sense; it involves the production of new forms of expression and it also invokes a clearly perceived "ideal listener."

> Dieser Zuhörer ist so zu sprechen der Vertreter der Menschheit, und ihn mitzuschaffen und das Gefühl seiner Gegenwart lebendig zu erhalten, ist vielleicht das Feinste und Stärkste, was die schöpferische Kraft des Prosaikers zu leisten hat" (PIV, 53)

> (This listener is, so to speak, the representative of mankind, and to help to create him, to preserve the vital sense of his presence, is perhaps the subtlest and most powerful thing to be achieved by the creative strength and the writer of prose.)

The crucial problem lies in the establishment of contact, in communication with the "idealer Zuhörer."[2] In other words,

---

2 The term ideal is used in its dual lexical meaning of "existing as an idea or archetype," and therefore imagined, as well as "perceived as perfect in its kind" (Oxford English Dictionary).

it becomes a problem of language and style and to this problem we shall continually be returning. The idea that writing consists above all in communicating, that it both envisages and addresses a reader and in so doing creates him, that is a social activity with what he saw as a convivial function ("gesellig" is a term much favored by Hofmannsthal); this idea is one which gradually evolves until it has grown into a conviction. Hofmannsthal saw the spoken word, either in the theater or in life, as a preeminently social medium; "die Rede als soziales Element, als *das* soziale Element" (A, 231, speech as a social element, as *the* social element). That is why the comedies, being a distillation of social intercourse, represent for the writer "das erreichte Soziale" (A, 226, the social ideal attained).

What I here aim to provide is something like an outline of the growth of that consciousness in Hofmannsthal towards an ever securer appraisal of the writer's role as one who addresses himself to others. It is a development he was later to see critically as a shift of emphasis from creative self-indulgence to conscious mediation. In a letter to Strauss, June 4, 1924, he recalls: "Vieles, das ich in aller Einsamkeit der Jugend hervorgebracht hatte, völlig für mich, selbst an den Leser kaum denkend, waren phantastische kleinen Opern und Singspiele ohne Musik." (Much that I produced in the solitude of youth, completely for myself, with scarcely a thought even about readers, were fantastic little operas and libretti without music). Language as "das gesellige Element, worin sich beide, der Redende und der Angeredete, zusammen wissen" (PIV, 434 the convivial element in which both the speaker and the one spoken to feel they are together), is to figure as the focal area of attention. Hofmannsthal's life-long struggle with the complex problem of the word provides, in my view, the surest access to his creative personality, to his sense of purpose as well as to the growth of his mind and imagination. It is largely in his prose and of course in his letters that one must look for the most revealing insights into his creative self.

The question "for whom do I write?" is quite explicit in a number of places throughout. Hofmannsthal's writings, it figures, for instance, in a late diary entry of November 1, 1926 which barely alludes to the confessional element in *Der Kaiser und die Hexe* (*The Emperor and the Witch*) and then becomes introverted as a motive is sought for writing the diary itself:

> Auch diese Seiten selbst sind Bekenntnis. Und für wen schreib ich sie – für wen dürfte ich sie ohne Eitelkeit schreiben? Auch hier bedarf es einer Geisterbeschwörung: empirische Begegnungen müssen vergeistigt werden" (A, 238)

> (These pages too are a confession, And for whom do I write them – for whom might I write them without being vain? In this too, a summoning up of spirits is needed: empirical encounters must be made spiritual.)

The words appear somewhat inscrutable at first and may need some explanation. On the same pages Hofmannsthal reflects on the virtual impossibility of anyone being able to write his biography. He likens the task to the summoning of the spirit of Samuel by the witch of Endor at Saul's command (I Samuel 28).

"Es handelt sich, den Geist der Epoche und den des Individuums zu beschwören und sie beide auseinanderzuhalten. Die Hexe von Endor ist schließlich erschöpft und halb tot" (A, 238 It is a question of summoning up the spirit of an era and of an individual and to draw them asunder. The witch of Endor is finally exhausted and half dead.) The analogy of this "Geisterbechwörung," then, suggests nothing short of the miraculous. The potential biographer of Hofmannsthal is forewarned. We know from his discussion of the art of biography "Der Schatten der Lebenden" ("The Shadow of the Living") how rare is the recreative gift which he termed "die mimische Kraft" (the mimic power) or again "mimische Sympathie" (mimic sympathy) in a theatrical figure of speech. This capacity, shared by actor, dramatist and painter alike, enables them to enter into the living image and act out its life in their particular medium. One might justifiably consider Hofmannsthal's occasional diary entries and notes contained in the volume *Aufzeichnungen* (*Notes*) as a fragmentary inner autobiography written with some purposive communication in mind. The need for some kind of affirmation or acknowledgement is clearly evident in his reference to personal vanity. It surely reveals the writer's inability to practice his gift without envisaging a public of some kind.[3]

The practice, however, is thwarted by innumerable inhibitions

---

3   Hermann Rudolph in his study *Kulturkritik und konservative Revolution*, Tübingen: Niemeyer, 1971, p. 197, puts the date at which Hofmannsthal begins by design to influence a public at around the turn of the century.

and they are all ultimately of a kind which involves the functions of language. So much of the reticence in the later Hofmannsthal springs from a refined sense of the fitness of words, an extreme sensibility to nuance in all verbal communication. These qualities are raised to the level of sophisticated comedy – indeed one might say they are successfully laughed off – when embodied in the figure of Hans Karl. He confesses to Crescence:

> "Mir können über eine Dummheit die Tränen in die Augen kommen – oder es wird mir heiß vor gène über eine ganze Kleinigkeit, über eine Nuance, die kein Mensch merkt, oder es passiert mir, daß ich ganz laut sag, was ich mir denk – das sind doch unmögliche Zuständ, um unter Leut zu gehen." (LII, 154)

> (I may get tears in my eyes over some silly matter – or else I grow hot with embarrassment over a tiny little thing, over a nuance which no one notices; or it may happen that I say something I am thinking out loud – surely these are impossible circumstances for going about meeting people.)

The delicacy of the relationship between speaker and language, language and society, is nicely captured. Hans Karl's frequent lapses into silence and the much less determinate language of gesture are his principle means of beating a retreat from the indiscretions of social intercourse. Transferred to the context of the writer in his public role, these inhibitions lose none of their sting. There is a striking affinity of idea in a reflection in the *Buch der Freunde* (*The Book of Friends*) which clearly carries personal accents:

"Die Scham von seinen eigensten Verhältnissen zu niemand reden zu wollen, ist eine Selbstwarnung des Gemütes; in jedes Geständnis, in jede Darstellung schließt sich leicht die Verzerrung ein, und aus dem Zartesten, Unsagbaren wird im Handumdrehen das Gemeine" (A, 25)

(The sense of shame which hinders one from speaking out one's innermost experiences is a self-warning signal of the sentient mind; distortion easily intrudes into every confession, every description, and the most delicate, unutterable thing is in an instant turned into the vulgar.)

The dangerous proximity of "das Geistige" to "das Gemeine" is a fundamental realization. The deep-seated awareness of, and sensitivity to, the distortions effected by words when ineptly used is a constant preoccupation of Hofmannsthal's writing. It is, of course, repeatedly introduced into *Der Schwierige*, especially into the dialogues involving Agathe and Edine who both have an unfailing gift for creating "das Gemeine" despite their more delicate aspirations. "Das Wort ist mächtiger als der es spricht" (The word is mightier than the one who utters it) states one of the last aphorisms in *Buch der Freunde* (A, 84), and like most fundamental ideas in Hofmannsthal it has reference to both the comic and the serious aspects of his writing.

It is an idea already developed in the essay about Mitterwurzer, "Eine Monographie" ("A Monograph") of 1895, which contains some of his most perceptive comments on language. There we find the formulation: "für gewöhnlich stehen nicht die Worte in der Gewalt der Menschen, sondern die Menschen in der Gewalt der

Worte" (in general, words do not lie within the power of people, but people within the power of words). And who better to render account of the overwhelming power of words than the young poet Loris who later came to write "Ein Brief" ("A Letter"). In this essay Hofmannsthal's classicist loyalties come to the fore. The forgotten ideal of *elegantia*, practiced by the Platonists and their Renaissance successors, is contrasted with the modern distrust of "das gut Ausgedrückte" (that which is well expressed). Hofmannsthal diagnoses a weakness of intellectual and moral outlook (he uses the already discredited term "Gesinnung" – mentality) in a contemporary world of uncertain or illusory values whose impotence is especially noticeable in relation to language. For language can take over and exploit a particular ineptitude, the disregard for words – "die naïve Redekraft" (the naive power of speech) – and make the speaker its unsuspecting mouthpiece (an insight, incidentally, which the highly word-conscious plays of Horvath were later to explore to the full). Language is for Hofmannsthal the repository of tradition, bearing within it the memorable contributions of succeeding generations. No individual writer, he comes to believe, can produce something permanent without recourse to tradition.[4] This idea is contained in a striking, if somehow uncanny, metaphor: "Wenn wir den Mund aufmachen reden immer zehntausend Tote mit" (PI, 230 Whenever we open our mouth, ten thousand of the dead also speak). The same metaphor is retained in the late essay "Wert und Ehre deutscher Sprache" ("The Value and Honor of the German language") – one indication

---

4 Letter to Strauss, June 4, 1924 Hofmannsthal Strauss p. 505.

of that "formidable Einheit des Werkes" (formidable unity of my oeuvre) which he himself had noted (A, 237) – where he writes: "Die Sprache ist ein großes Totenreich, unausrottbar tief" (PIV, 439 Language is a great realm of the dead, too deep to sound out). The idea that language contains within it forces that can easily outstrip individual control is also formulated in a distich, oddly reminiscent of Hebbel, entitled "Eigene Sprache":

> Wuchs dir die Sprache im Mund, so wuchs in der Hand dir die Kette:
> Zieh nun das Weltall zu dir! Ziehe! Sonst wirst du gechleift (GLD, 102)
>
> (If language grew into your mouth, the chain also grew in your hand;
> Now pull the universe towards you! Pull! Or you will be dragged.)

The contest, a kind of tug-o-war between the cumulative power of language and its solitary user, appears to be an unequal one. The repeated imperative "ziehe" strikes one less as a note of confident strength than as a fearful warning.

The magic power exerted by words is the very groundwork of Hofmannsthal's creativity in the early period. The young Hofmannsthal writing "Poesie und Leben" (1896 "Poetry and Life") offers an image of the poet as one who is the thrall of words: "die schwebenden, die unendlich vieldeutigen, die zwischen Gott und Geschöpf hängenden Worte" (PI, 266 those hovering, endlessly ambiguous words which hang between God and his creature). Words, the material of poetry, assume an aura of independent life; their redolent and expressive power produces that undefined, vital "Wirkung" (effect) which is to him both the test and the justification of all art. "Ja denn ich halte Wirkung für die Seele der Kunst, für ihren Leib, für ihren Kern und ihre Schale, für ihr ganzes völliges Wesen" (PI, 266 Yes, for I hold effect to be the very soul of art, its body, its core and its shell, its entire consummate being). These are still unmistakably the views of aestheticism, a premise which recognizes an insuperable gulf between the language of poetry and the ordinary language of daily discourse. Hofmannsthal uses a memorable metaphor to express what is seen as a fixed relationship:

"Das Wort als Träger eines Lebensinhaltes und das traumhafte Bruderwort, welches in einem Gedicht stehen kann, streben auseinander und schweben fremd aneinander vorüber, wie die beiden Eimer eines Brunnens" (Pl, 263)

{The word as the carrier of some content of life and its brother, the dreamlike word which may be found in a poem, draw apart and hover past one another like to buckets of a well.)

This isolation of poetic language, which sets it apart and ascribes to it a wholly individual function and freedom, is here seen in a positive light; indeed, it is understood as the proper condition for the practicing poet. "Der eigene Ton ist alles" (Pl, 265 an individual tone is everything) is the mark of the true poet, so we are told. "Der Mutigste und der Stärkste ist der, der seine Worte am freisten zu stellen vermag; denn es ist nichts so schwer als sie aus ihren festen, falschen Verbindungen zu reißen" (Pl, 265

The boldest and the strongest man is the one who can most freely place his words; for nothing is so difficult as to tear them from their firm, false connections). There is disdain for the philologist, the newspaper journalist, and the "Scheindichter: – would be poet (who are called "staubfressende Geister") since each is seen as in some way destructive of the sense of form, that wholeness of response which the artist of words exemplifies. Stefan George is at this period singled out as one whose poetry is distinguished by the quality of selfness, of possessing "einen eigenen Ton" (Pl, 242 an individual tone) and despite their personal estrangement Hofmannsthal's respect for George the poet remained constant. In 1922 he was still paying public tribute to his strength of purpose: "Einem seichten Individualismus hat er den Begriff geistigen Dienens entgegengehalten" (PIV, 149 he opposed a shallow individualism with the concept of the service of the intellect). It is ironical therefore, in view of this common concern with service to the word, that the differences between them should largely have stemmed from what Hofmannsthal saw as his proper course as a man of letters, namely, his turn to the traditions of theater and to congenial prose forms in which he came to perfect his mature talent.

The public address is a form Hofmannsthal adopted on numerous occasions and this fact alone testifies to his abiding concern to communicate and maintain vital contact with a public. "Der Dichter und die Zeit (1907 "The Poet and Our Times"), written just over ten years after "Poesie und Leben," shows a much altered understanding of the writer and of his pubic role. We now find him reluctant to make the illiberal distinction between poets and would-be-poets (the scornful term "Scheindichter" used in the earlier speech has been discarded). He now maintains "diese haarscharfe Absonderung des Dichters vom Nicht-Dichter erscheint mir gar nicht möglich" (PII, 231 this very fine distinction between poet and non-poet seems to me quite impossible). Schematic notions of "the poet" are abandoned for subtler differentiations of level and degree. The idea is submitted that the poetic does not exist in isolated forms as a pure distillation but that elements of it may be found intermingled with other literary qualities.[5] He is equally reticent about any attempt to define what is meant by "die Gegenwart" (the present) or "die Epoche" (this era), preferring to use the tentative term "Atmosphäre" in generalization of intellectual temper of the day. Hofmannsthal inevitably turns to the suggestiveness of figurative language in order to create a vivid mental image (or a sort of working model) in illustration of an idea and come increasingly to distrust the very concept of "die Gegenwart" as wholly insubstantial and chimerical: "Es ist der Zustand fruchtbarer sinnlicher Gebundenheit, in welchen das neunzehnte Jahrhundert uns hineingeführt, woraus nun dieses Götzenbild 'Gegenwart' hervorsteigt" (PIV, 438 it is the condition of a terrible sensuous limitation, into which the nineteenth century had led us, out of which this idol of "the present" now arises). Elsewhere he asserts, "Das Wesen unserer Epoche ist Vieldeutigkeit und Unbestimmtheit" (PH, 235f the essence of our age is ambiguity and indefiniteness). The poet's relationship to his

---

5 Letter to George, June 18, 1902, Hofmannsthal George, p. 154.

times is therefore the more uncertain and yet Hofmannsthal gives a surprisingly hopeful rendering of this seeming lack of contact between poet and public. He establishes a firm image of contemporary man, suggestive of serious dedication to cultural values: "Ich sehe beinahe als die Geste unserer Zeit den Menschen mit dem Buch in der Hand: (PII, 237 I see this almost as a gesture of our times; Man with a book in his hand). The symbolic figure of this reader is interpreted as one whose ultimate, unconscious goal, whether by way of novel or newspaper, is an inner satisfaction which poetry alone can give: "die ganze Bezauberung der Poesie" (PII, 239 the whole enchantment of poetry). This reductive idea that all thirst for literature, all idle or genuine curiosity about books, all reading activity whatever form it may take, is in the last resort a quest for the language of poetry, an incipient attempt to reach for the deepest levels of linguistic experience, may possibly be found presumptuous. But it is a poet who writes and he writes without a hint of arrogance. Respect for and dedication to "das mächtige Geheimnis der Sprache" (the mighty mystery of language) in every line of this prose. So far from adopting a condescending tone towards indifferent writing, he attempts to establish connections between forms of language in all cultural levels, remarking upon precedents, affinities and gradations. Thus it is that, despite the poet's undisputed remoteness, some small part of his art finds its way into the most casual or trivial act of reading; the half-read newspaper thrust into the laborer's shirt or the penny-dreadful handed round behind the shop counter. The line of descent from masterpiece to hack novel, no matter how devious or obscure, is acknowledged as valid, it is a position pleaded for, it seems to me, with more vehemence than conviction. The note of cultural optimism sounds strained and anxious in this product of the middle years before the Great War, that acid test of civilized values, broke out.

The poet's existence in the contemporary world is likened to Ulysses returning unrecognized to his own in the humblest guise; the possessor of all, despised by all. He is seen as intimately involved in the processes and conflicts of his age – the familiar metaphors of the magician, the chameleon, the mirror, the diver, the seismograph, are applied to him by turn – and this involvement is depicted as a passive condition of suffering and receptivity ("Dies Leidend-Genießen" – this state of pain cum pleasure – as it is ambivalently called). The poet is by virtue of his natural gift, wholly responsive to his time and therefore the fullest embodiment of his time: "in ihm oder nirgends ist Gegenwart" (PH, 245 the present is in him or it is nowhere). But there remains the insistent theme of estrangement and isolation – that lack of communication between the poet and the contemporary world which Hofmannsthal continually tried to bridge – which attends the exploration of living contact. Hofmannsthal cannot express the intuition that the creative literature to which he is dedicated, and of which he can securely use the terms "Poesie" or "Dichtung" (poetry or creative writing), is not necessarily a shared possession even with the audience he is addressing. This profound doubt as to common ground of consent is plainly voiced at the end of the speech:

"denn Sie sitzen vor mir, viele Menschen, und ich weiß nicht, zu wem ich rede: aber ich rede nur für die, die mit mir gehen wollen, und nicht für den, der sich sein Wort gegeben hat, dies alles von sich abzulehnen. Ich kann nur für die reden, für die Gedichtetes da ist. Die, durch deren Dasein die Dichter erst ein Leben bekommen, Denn sie sind ewig Antwortende, und ohne die Fragenden ist der Antwortende ein Schatten" (PII, 255f)

(for you, many people, sit here in front of me and I do not know to whom I am speaking: yet I speak only for those who wish to go along with me and not for anyone who has agreed in his heart to reject all of this. I can only speak for those for whom poetry actually exists; for those by whose existence alone the poets acquire life. For they are ever the ones who respond, and without those who ask the responder is a shadow.)

One can hardly miss the defensive note of appeal in this solitary voice. This is not the style of self-certainty but one which attempts to enlist sympathy, to plead its cause. The reciprocity of the poet as "der Antwortende" as the public as "die Fragenden" is a rhetorical contrivance rather than an idea that can be validated. The allusive, visionary mode of language used throughout, however evocative, cannot quite disguise the doubt it hopes to allay. The concluding image of the ideal reader as "der Überwinder der Zeit" (the conqueror of time) who is captured by the poetic vision as though by a religious experience, can scarcely be identified with that typified figure of the times with which Hofmannsthal began: a man standing book in hand. This ideal reader of 1907 rather too closely resembles the poet himself and he must share in the poet's solitude.

Hofmannsthal's preoccupation with the role of the poet as the spokesman of culture is shared by such important writers of the age as W. B. Yeats and Alexander Blok, both of whom wrote essays and speeches close in spirit to him and often reminiscent of his own. Yeats may write with more assured accents in his role of mediator between a people and its literary traditions, Blok's voice may be more strident, zealous and impatient for change, but each shares with Hofmannsthal's a particular pathos and urgency born of the historical moment. They share the concern to renew and interpret a literary heritage for the nation, the wish to communicate to their respective people an image of the poet which would be familiar, accessible and meaningful. Blok especially took a prophetic role in the words he addressed to the nation from 1907 until the year of his death in 1921 in essays such as "Religious Quests and the People," "Art and Revolution," "The People and the Intelligentsia." Blok aligned himself with "the simple man" of the people and not with the intelligentsia who had divided the artist from the people and had created hostility between them. He too believed, more passionately than Hofmannsthal and with a surer sense of their needs, in the people's thirst for art and literature. His public oratory is terser and more direct, his tone less tentative, less speculative than Hofmannsthal's, whose elegant formulations are knowingly addressed to the cultured and like-minded. In his speech "The People and the Intelligentsia" delivered to educated audiences at the end of 1908, Blok reveals his sense of mission by communicating in a language that is fresh and vigorous and lacking in all literary self-consciousness.[6] It is not a rarefied language of the cultured classes but belongs to the people from which it came. Moreover, Blok is not concerned with the phenomenon of the problem of language – therein lies the major distinction from Hofmannsthal – but with ideas: with the gulf in understanding between the people and the intelligentsia, with the history of that division and its possible resolutions.

For Hofmannsthal the very language available to the German writer in itself presented a problem of culture. The consciousness of far-reaching differences of meaning attributed to the term "Literatur" in German as compared with neighboring countries finds fullest expression in "Das Schrifttum als geistiger Raum der Nation" ("Literature as the Intellectual Domain of the Nation"). The idea that literature of a nation should be co-extensive with its entire culture, should consummately embrace its intellectual, social and historical life and be a perpetual reminder of the reality of that life, is found to be true of the French but not of the Germans. For the French term "literature" embraces "das Große," "das Mittlere" as well as "das Geringe" (the great; the midway, the lesser). What Hofmannsthal finds lacking in German is that "mittlere Sprache" (middle language) which binds all parts of a nation, a "Sprachnorm" (language norm) which represents the confluence of all literary tendencies in a culture. Hofmannsthal has repeatedly drawn attention to the solitariness of German literary genius ("der leidenschaflich-einsame Dienst an der eigenen

---

6 To the Religious-Philosophical Society on November 4, and to the Literary Society of St. Petersburg on December 12, 1908.

Seele" PIV, 409 – the passionate and solitary service to one's own soul), to the lack of a tradition, to the absence of a recognized canon such as the French possess (PIV, 133). In reading other languages with empathy, he appreciated particularly the cultural cohesion they express and is put in mind of that quality of resistance peculiar to German; a resistance which only the greatest poets could overcome: "unsere höchsten Dichter allein, möchte man sagen gebrauchen unsere Sprache sprachgemäß – ob auch die Schriftsteller bleibt fraglich" (PIV, 437 Only our poets of the highest standing, one is tempted to say, employ our language in accordance with its genius – if the writers do so too remains questionable). The essay "Wert und Ehre deutscher Sprache" (1927) is particularly sensitive to this problem of both recalcitrance and vital potential in the language. Hofmannsthal recognizes in German no solid middle ground, no valid "mittlere Sprache" or "correct style" as the secure possession of a tradition of letters: "man kann nur individuell schreiben, oder man schreibt schon schlecht" (PIV, 434f one can only write individually, or one begins to write badly).[7] The true identity of the nation can be discovered only in "den hohen Sprachdenkmälern und in den Volksdialekten"

---

7 It is very likely that Hofmannsthal's formulation derives from Ludwig Börne's essay "Bemerkungen über Sprache und Styl" which is strikingly similar in many points. In making the same distinction between good prose style in Germany and in France Börne writes: "Wer in Frankreich schreibt, schreibt wie die guten französischen Schriftsteller, oder schreibt schlecht" (whoever writes in France, writes in the manner of the good French writers, or else wrote badly), in Ludwig Börne, *Gesammelte Schriften*, Hamburg and Frankfurt am Main: Hofmann & Campe, 1862, vol. 1, pp. 18-19.

(PIV, 435 in the high literary monuments and in national dialects). The language of the Viennese popular theater is accordingly recognized in the essay on Ferdinand Raimund as an achieved synthesis of contrasting elements, a medium fully expressive of its culture: "eine barocke Sprache, eine Mischung aus dem Höheren und dem Niederen, halb großer Stil, halb die Sprache des wienerischen Hanswurst" (PIII, 475 a baroque language, a mixture of the higher and lower, in part grand style, in part the language of the Viennese stage clown). The difficulty of aspiring to high literary excellence in German finds subtle expression in a reflection contained in the prose piece "Reise im nördlichen Afrika" (1925 "Travels in Northern Africa"):

> "Wie die hohe Sprache bei uns aufsteigt ins unheimlich Geistige, kaum mehr von den Sinnen Beglänzte, und wie der Sprachsinn dann müde herabsinkt ins Gemeine, oder sich in den Dialekt zurückschmiegen muß, um nur wieder die Erde zu fühlen – und dazwischen ein Abgrund. Wie jeder sich die Sprache neu schaffen muß und nicht weiß, ob er noch tut, was er darf, oder schon ins Müßige, Künstliche gerät, und jeder in diesem Tun jeden bezweifelt und befeindet und oft auch sich selber, und wie die Sprache doch durch die Herrlichkeit ihrer Aufschwünge und Offenbarungen wieder alles Erlittene aufwiegt." (PIV, 259)

> (How our elevated language rises up to the uncanny reaches of the intellect, scarcely illumined by the senses, and how the feel for language then wearily lapses into ordinariness or has to fall back upon dialect, if only to feel the earth again – and in between there lies an abyss. How each one has to create his own language afresh and is uncertain whether he is still doing what is permissible

or has already slipped into the casual, the artificial; and how everyone directs doubt or hostility towards everyone else or towards himself in the process, and how the language can once more make good all of its losses by its glorious soaring flights and revelations.)

The metaphor of gravity and aspiring flight is full of stress and strenuousness suggestive of this struggle carried on by the writer in his effort to find his appropriate medium. In the absence of a well-tried tradition of *belles-lettres*, there are no smooth transitions (which Hofmannsthal termed "glatte Fügung" PIV, 433 – even juncture) available to the writer but only a deep divide between the language of "Dichtung" and the more mundane forms of writing.

Hofmannsthal was persistent in his attempts to identify a language of common discourse in which the nation could meet. Already in the essay "Umrisse eines neuen Journalismus" (1907 "Outlines of a new Journalism") we find him exploring the question of where that middle ground of language might lie: "diese so schwer als leicht zu handhabende Kunstform, dieser ernsthafte, loyale und unpedantische Journalismus" (PII, 260 this art form which is both difficult and easy to manage; this earnest, dependable and unpedantic journalism). It might well strike one as a strange aberration in one whose judgments on matters of style are so reliable, that Heine should be found objectionable as a literary model in precisely this area: Heine, who, more than any preceding writer, pioneered and perfected that worldly-wise, responsible and versatile prose style which established itself in modern journalism. On more than one occasion he draws attention to the dangerous influence of Heine's language on German letters (once referred to in a poem as "verfänglich Blendwerk" (GLD, 107 – suspect delusion).[8] Hofmannsthal evidently distrusted the nature of this pervasive irony and felt insecure about its aims (PI, 20). It was certainly neither "ernsthaft" nor "loyal" in its tenor. He looked rather to those he called "kulturelle Journalisten" (PII, 262 cultural journalists), writers like H. G. Wells. Goldsworthy Lowes Dickinson, Lafcadio Hearn and Maurice Barrès, who combined qualities of sound learning, intellect and good taste in their entertaining and readable prose. Above all it was Bernard Shaw who appeared to him as the man of the moment – "vielleicht die repräsentativste Figur des Augenblicks (perhaps the most representative figure of the moment) as he wrote in 1921 (PIV, 76); a writer who commanded an idiom (or "Jargon" as Hofmannsthal preferred to call it) exactly attuned to the intellectual climate of the day; an ironic intelligence responsive to a scientific age full of bewildering absurdities. Shaw, the incorrigible ironist, is seen as Heine's natural heir. This connection is most revealing of Hofmannsthal's literary and philosophical criteria. Shaw, and by implication Heine, are not felt to offer answers to the deepest religious concerns of the age, and Hofmannsthal is using the phrase "religiöse Bindungen" (PIV, 76 religious bonds) in the most generous sense as an existential need. It is Dostoevsky who fulfills this need most completely and is recognized as the dominant spiritual influence of the age: "er stößt durch die soziale Schilderung hindurch ins Absolute, ins Religiöse" (PIV, 77 he penetrates beyond social depiction into the

---

8 Cf. PI, 189; PII, 260; PIV, 76.

sphere of the absolute, the religious). Irony shows scant respect for absolutes and Hofmannsthal clearly sees its shortcomings in treating the most serious questions. Rather than welcome the ironist as an important contributor to the middle ground of the literary language which he felt German to be lacking, he takes his stand on austerely purist premises.

It is characteristic of the later Hofmannsthal whilst planning a literary monthly, later to be realized as *Neue deutsche Beiträge* (*New German Contributions*) that the emphasis is not on a contemporary image or style. On the contrary, a severely conservative concept is drawn up:

> Durchaus entgegen dem Zeitgeist, der negiert wird. Keine Jagd nach dem ungreifbaren Momentanen: der Begriff des Aktuellen als unvorhanden betrachtet. (A, 367)

> (Decidedly contrary to the spirit of the times, which is negated. Not a hunt for what is intangible and momentary; the idea of the topical considered non-existent.)

Furthermore, the essay which is rather harshly termed "die alles verschlingende Unform" (all-devouring formlessness) is to be banished from the project. The flexibility and inclusiveness of the essay form, instead of being considered advantageous, is viewed with suspicion; it is one "der alles vermischt und verfälscht" (A, 368 which mingles and trivializes everything). Here it is a case of the conceived idea prevailing over practical considerations of an imagined readership. The ideal reader is replaced by an abstraction, by a rarified principle called "ein höheres Soziales" (a higher social element). In this instance we see Hofmannsthal at his most uncompromising, directing a gesture of defiance, as it were, at literary anarchy. In the post-war years his activities are increasingly directed towards an end which was both idealist and practical; the creation of a cultured public responsive to the great legacy of German literature and theater. His collaboration with Max Reinhardt in founding the "Salzburger Festspiele" is a significant part of that endeavor.

Hofmannsthal was acutely aware of the fragmented and threatened nature of post-war European civilization and the several great anthologies he produced can be seen as an act of cultural unification and restoration. The *Deutsches Lesebuch* (*German Reader*) published by the Bremer Presse in 1922 summarizes a century of great writing from Lessing to Stifter and is conceived as a worthy counterpart to the celebrated age of French classicism. In the preface Hofmannsthal shows exact awareness of his reader: "den in seiner Einbildungskraft mitzuschaffen die oberste gesellige Pflicht dessen ist, der ein Buch macht" (IV, 1139 f, to create whom in his own imagination, is the foremost convivial duty of the writer of any book). This reader is envisaged as one who is not merely moved by an historical curiosity but one who, like Hofmannsthal, has a lively sense of what is of permanent value and is able to assimilate the traditions of the past into the present. This intercommunication between past and present, "das Ewige" and "das Gegenwärtige" (the eternal; the present-day) which is pursued to the point of their identification (PIV, 438), provides the basic principle for his anthologies. The reader is invited to discover this inner unity for himself and thus to fashion his own links with the past. The question "An wen aber wenden sich diese Sammlungen?" (to whom are these collections addressed?) is presented in "Wert und Ehre deutscher Sprache" (PIV, 440). The consciousness of a far-flung readership, unpredictable and disparate in their response to the literary legacy of the nation, is anxiously expressed.

It is most revealing that in the year 1922 we find Hofmannsthal once again taking up the idea of the literary circle; an idea he had emphatically disowned in his correspondence with George twenty years past, as one foreign to his freer literary associations.[9] He even reverts to a terminology which distinctly echoes that correspondence: "Der Wille zu geistigem Dienst gleichfalls ist das Zusammenhaltende des Kreises, den wir hier ankündigen" (PIV, 149, the will to intellectual service is equally the binding element for the circle which we here announce). Hofmannsthal's awareness of the threat to what remained of a fragmented culture is perhaps the direst experience of his last years. Nonetheless he is unwilling to renounce the hope that the core of the nation remains responsive to his restorative purpose. The suffering figure of Sigismund in *Der Turm* (*The Tower*), is the tragic symbol of that fragile hope.

Solitude as the writer's native element is an abiding idea in Hofmannsthal, though, as I have attempted to show, it carries different meaning at various stages of his development. At first solitude is conceived as the *donné* of the practicing poet who works within a medium separated from other forms of language.

---

9 Letter to George July 24, 1902, Hofmannsthal George, p. 164.

In the middle years the emphasis shifts to a more liberal view; the intuitive recognition that the poet, however seemingly remote, is in some sense present in all forms of language. Finally, the will to create cohesion, to discover wholeness, to explore linguistic and cultural norms, is an attempt to surmount the deeply felt divisions of language as the index and symbol of a society's culture.

The voluminous and varied correspondences Hofmannsthal carried on with friends and literary associates throughout his life, represent yet another important means of overcoming the solitude of his vocation. They have been called "fast ein selbstständiges Oeuvre" (almost an independent oeuvre) in a searching paper by Richard Exner and evaluated as the most significant transitions between life and works.[10] They are so in a further important sense if viewed from the particular relationship I have been discussing; that of author to public. For the correspondent is, in the truest sense, Hofmannsthal's "idealer Zuhörer"; not an imagined but a chosen reader, a mind often congenial to his own, both receptive and responsive, unfamiliar at first but increasingly known, not merely a passive listener but an answering voice and one who proves essential in the enduring process of the writer's self-discovery. From the early correspondence with Bebenburg, to whom he was both friend and mentor, to the last exchanges with Rilke whose development he observed with a mixture of admiration and reserve, we find Hofmannsthal turning the exchange to

---

10 Richard Exner, "Hofmannsthal heute? (Eine Rede)" MAL, vol. 10, no. 2, 1977, p. 20.

advantage, preserving and confirming his creative freedom.[11]

That he never lost the sense of contact with the reader or audience, never ceased to be concerned with the writer's need to communicate is, as I hope to have indicated, amply attested. When in conclusion to his preface to the *Deutsches Lesebuch*, he wrote, "ein Buch ist zur größeren Hälfte des Lesers Werk, wie ein Theater des Zuschauers" (PIV, 141 a book is in greater part the work of the reader, as theater is that of the spectator), he was placing his faith in that vital alliance between creativity and receptivity, experiment and criticism, without which no culture can grow into tradition. Indeed, Hofmannsthal dignified his ideal listener with the highest of expectations. If we return to our opening premise and the essay "Schöne Sprache" we find a description of this listener which raises him to convivial partnership with the writer:

"Denn dieser Zuhörer muß so zartfühlend, so schnell

---

11 Rolf Tarot, *Hugo von Hofmannsthal: Daseinsformen und dichterische Struktur*, Tübingen: Niemeyer, 1970, p. 139 asserts that the letters contain "eine spontan zutage tretende Selbstdarstellung des Dichters" (a spontaneous form of self-depiction by the poet), but is not concerned to investigate the writer's notion of style or his specific interest in communicating with a reader; the conscious act of addressing himself to others. Johannes Arnoldus Heberle's early thesis *Hofmannsthal: Beobachtungen über seinen Stil*, Enschede: Van der Loeff, 1937, and above all Hermann Broch's *Gesammelte Werke*, vol. 6, "Essays 1," Zurich: Rhein, 1955 have proved almost without successors in this area until the recent study by William E. Yates, *Schnitzler, Hofmannsthal and the Austrian Theater*, New Haven and London: Yale University Press, 1992, which gives fullest weight of attention to Hofmannsthal's letters as a source of illumination for both biography and work.

in der Auffassung, so unbestechlich im Urteil, so fähig zur Aufmerksamkeit, so Kopf und Herz in eins gedacht werden, daß er fast über dem zu stehen scheint, der zu ihm redet, oder es wäre nicht der Mühe wert, für ihn zu schreiben." (PIV, 53)

(For this listener must be thought of as so sensitive, so quick in his grasp, so incorruptible in judgment, so capable of attention, so united in head and heart, that he almost seems to stand above the one who addresses him, else it would not be worth the trouble to write for him.)

Few authors have paid so gracious a compliment to their readers.

Milton Keynes UK
Ingram Content Group UK Ltd.
UKHW022011260424
441792UK00012B/93/J